The Sign in Matthew 24

By: Philip Mitanidis

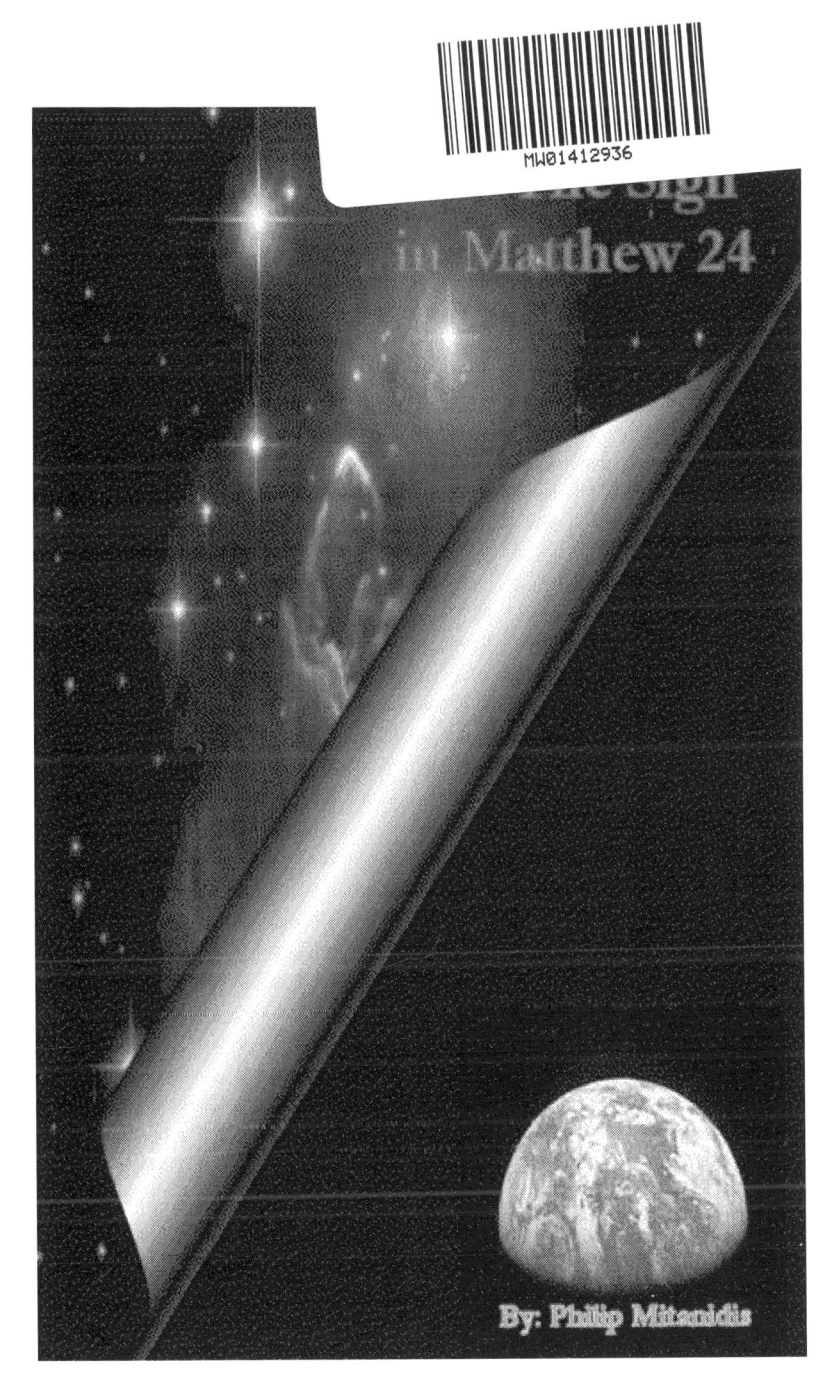

"The Sign"

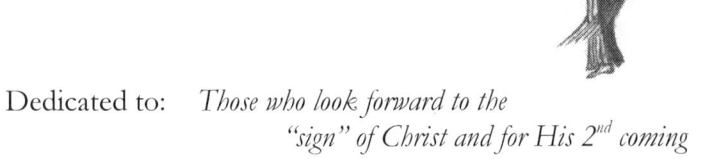

Dedicated to: *Those who look forward to the "sign" of Christ and for His 2nd coming*

Copyright © 2014 by Philip Mitanidis
All Rights Reserved

All rights reserved. No part of this publication may be reproduced or transmitted in any form or by any means, electronically, or mechanically, including photocopy, recording, or by any information storage and retrieving system without written permission from the publisher.

For further information or request for permission to make copies of any part of the work should be in a written form and mailed to the following address:

To contact us:
BEEHIVE PUBLISHING HOUSE INC.
e-mail: thehive@beehivepublishinghouse.com
www.beehivepublishinghouse.com

The Sign in Matthew 24
First Edition 2014. Printed in the USA.
ISBN 978-0-9866246-5-0

Published work by Philip Mitanidis:

The Creator of Genesis 1:1—Who is He?
The Covenant—A Contract Rejected
No God and Saviour Beside Me
According to a Promise
Christians Headed Into the Time of Trouble
Ghosts Demons UFO'S and Dead Men
Moses Wrote About Me
Blasphemies Against the Holy Ghost
What is the Sign of Christ's Second Coming and
    the End of the World
The Sign in Matthew 24
The Apostasy

IV___ ACKNOWLEDGEMENTS & ABBREVIATIONS

In my references from the Old King James Version (OKJV) Bible, I have changed the first letter of the pronouns into capital letters, which refer to God the Creator; and I have translated the Hebrew word "יהוה" and the Greek word "Κυριος" to read, in the upper casing, "LORD," whenever the Scriptures refer to God the Creator of Genesis 1:1.

Please refer to the Hebrew and to the Greek inspired Scriptures in order to verify my opinions.

All Bible references are given from the Old King James Version (OKJV) unless otherwise indicated.

Greek Scripture references are quoted from Η Αγια Γραφη, Βιβλικη Εταιρεια, Αθηναι 1961.

"Scripture quotations taken from THE AMPLIFIED BIBLE (Amp.), Copyright © 1954, 1958, 1962, 1964, 1965, 1987 by The Lockman Foundation. All rights reserved. Used by permission. (www.Lockman.org)"

"Scriptures quoted marked (CEV) are from t*he Contemporary English Version* Copyright © 1991, 1992, 1995 by American Bible Society. Used by permission.

Today's English Version (TEV). Copyright © 1992. American Bible Society, 1865 Broadway, New York, NY 10023. Used by permission

Picture in the "sign" is provided by NASA.
Map provided by SDA Bible commentary volume 8 p.556
Front & back covers produced by Philip Mitanidis.
The artwork in this book is produced by the Author Philip Mitanidis.

Foreword
===

Have you ever stopped to think how many times you have read the word "**sign**" in Matthew twenty-four and always understood it to mean "signs"? And do you recall how many times you have discussed that chapter with a friend, and always referred to the "sign," in regards to Jerusalem and to the "sign," in regards to the 2nd coming of Christ in the plural form? And do you remember if your friend ever corrected you for using the word "sign" in the plural form? Could the reason be because your friend believes that the word "sign," for some reason or another, reads "signs"! And how many times have you heard your pastor give a sermon on the second coming of Jesus Christ the LORD, and noted that he too is referring to the "sign" in the plural form?

But, perhaps you should not feel bad because, as you well know, the majority of people and men of the cloth refer to the word "sign," in Matthew 24, as signs. In fact, in contradiction to Christ's presentation of the word "sign," they take the liberty to go on and describe the "sign" in numerous ways when there is no description provided in Matthew 24 by Jesus Christ the LORD or by Apostle Matthew. And yet, pastors, lay workers, and religious leaders, when they refer to the "sign" of Matthew 24:30, they describe it as multiple signs, such as earthquakes, famine, wars, mega fires, pestilence, pandemic, typhoons, multiple tornados, mega destructive weather, etc., etc., that would take place before Jesus comes the 2nd time. In addition, they quote Matthew 24:4-12 to support the above comments. And even worse, they leave you with the impression that the description of the multiple signs is the "sign" of

Matthew 24:30!

But, that is not what Jesus said. And neither what Apostle Matthew wrote.

He wrote:

> "30 And then shall appear the sign of the Son of man in heaven: and then shall all the tribes of the earth mourn, and they shall see the Son of man coming in the clouds of heaven with power and great glory." Matthew 24:30

Jesus is quite clear in the above verse, He says, "30 And then shall appear the **sign** of the Son of man in heaven:" (v.30). He does not say "signs." Christ is specific; He says, "sign," and that is a big difference from what you have heard, what you hear from the pulpit, Radio, TV, what you have read, or what your friends tell you.

So! Why are pastors, teachers, men of the cloth, and religious leaders bent on describing the "sign" of Christ as "signs"? And why is the "sign" of Christ mostly referred to as some form of an event that takes place on earth, instead of "heaven"? And, why is the "sign" referred to as the 2nd coming of Christ the LORD? And why is such an important event explained away without scriptural support?

Perhaps to some, who explain the two signs of Matthew 24 away, as each event having multiple signs, is not important to them. But, you as a Christian, the "sign" of Christ should be important to you, as the "sign" for the destruction of Jerusalem and the Sanctuary was important to the apostles because the "sign" affected them as the "sign" of Christ, which would warn you and me of Christ's 2nd coming, affects us both. And, if you love Christ the LORD, and the well being of your fellow men and women, you too should be concerned because it affects them also.

You see, the apostles wanted to know about the two signs because they were told by Jesus to go and preach His Gospel message. And by preaching Christ's Gospel message, it meant that they were to go and warn the people in Jerusalem that the city was going to be destroyed; and if they wanted to escape death, they were to watch for the "sign." And when they saw the "sign," they were to drop everything they were doing and leave the city as quickly as possible.

And, in regards to the second "sign" (Matthew 24:30), the apostles are warning us today through their written pages. Therefore when the people see, after the "great tribulation," the "sign" of Christ "in heaven," they would know that Christ's second coming is around the corner. And by knowing what the "sign" of Christ looks like, and when it is going to appear, it gives a person the confidence that any proclamation by anyone in the world that Christ has come, prior to the appearing of the "sign" of Christ would be false, and should not be heeded or believed. For anyone to be claiming that Christ is here or there or in a secret chamber, Christ warns, do not believe "them." And when Satan the devil appears here and there proclaiming to be Christ, do not believe him. And when Satan tries to convince you that he is Christ by healing people and telling you deceptive lies do not believe him because the "sign" of Jesus Christ has not appeared in heaven for all the world to see. Therefore for anyone claiming to be Christ prior to the appearing of the "sign" of Christ would be a false Christ. And by you knowing these few facts, they can prevent you from being misled and deceived by Satan or by his satanic agencies.

By presenting you with the above few facts, now you can see why it is important to know what the "sign" of Christ looks like, when it will appear, and where it would appear. By knowing at least these few facts, you can find comfort like the people in Jerusalem who were watching for the "sign" to appear before the destruction of Jerusalem took place; and when it did, they escaped unscathed. By watching for the "sign" of Christ, you too can escape the deceptions that are going to take place before the "sign" of Christ takes place for every person on earth to see.

Therefore I strongly recommend that you read this book and listen carefully to the literal statements Jesus made about His "sign." Learn when the "sign" of Christ will take place, what the "sign" of Christ looks like, what events are going to take place, before the "sign" of Christ appears and after the "sign" of Christ appears, which will lead us to the appearing of Christ's 2nd coming. And learn how you will be able to escape the satanic deceptions and remain steadfast and saved in Christ the LORD of hosts, and bound for His eternal kingdom where there is eternal never-ending happiness and contentment.

The Author.

CONTENTS

Foreword..5
Contents...9
The Prediction...10
The Question...12
The Second Question..................................31
The first Angel's Message...........................38
    This Gospel......................................38
    The Judgment....................................42
    Worship Him that Made Heaven and earth........44
Unwarranted Objections..............................46
The Great Tribulation................................58
The "Sign" of Christ.................................117
Appendix..158
Questions...161
Bibliography...164

<u>Please note:</u> This book is not sent out to condemn the beliefs of men and women; it is written to warn, edify, and to simply allow Jesus Christ the LORD of hosts and Apostle John to reveal the "**sign**" of Christ and the sequence of events, to all of the people in the world, before Christ comes the second time with all of His angels, to planet earth, to take His people to the third heaven.

The Prediction

On Wednesday morning, 12, 31 AD, two days before Jesus Christ was crucified, He and His disciples arrived in Jerusalem from Simon the leper's house; and, as His custom was, Jesus went in the temple teaching the people His Gospel and revealing the errors of the priests and the errors of the leaders of the House of Judah, which they did not like Him doing. They preferred to banish Him completely from Jerusalem. But because of the people, they refrained from preventing Him going to the Temple (Sanctuary), seizing Him, or even prosecuting Him for fear of retaliation by the people who followed Him. We are told, "38 And all the people came early in the morning to Him in the temple, for to hear Him" (Luke 21:36-38). And when Jesus Christ finished teaching and healing people, He would leave the Temple, and the Temple area, normally late in the afternoon.

And, as Jesus was leaving the Temple area, some people were talking about the Temple and "5 how it was adorned with goodly stones and gifts" (Luke 21:5). And, as the conversation was going on about the Temple by some people, one of the disciples picked up on the conversation and said to Jesus, "1 see what manner of stones and what buildings are here!" (Mark 13:1).

In response, "2 Jesus answering said unto him, Seest thou [you] these great buildings? there shall not be left one stone upon another, that shall not be thrown down" (Mark 13:2). And turning to the rest of the disciples, to make sure that they all understood what He said, to their surprise, Jesus said to them, "6 As for these things which ye [all of you] behold, the days will come, in the which there shall not be left one stone

The Prediction

upon another, that shall not be thrown down" (Luke 21:6). Jesus not only knew what the buildings were made of, but also knew when they were going to be destroyed, when the walls of Jerusalem were going to be destroyed, by whom, what will happen to the people in Jerusalem, and to the Temple (Sanctuary).

After making His point, Jesus and His disciples left the temple area, and meandered through the city toward the northeast gate of Jerusalem, down to the Kidron Valley, and made His way up to Mount Olives, as He had done so many times before, to relax or to sleep there (Luke 21:37)

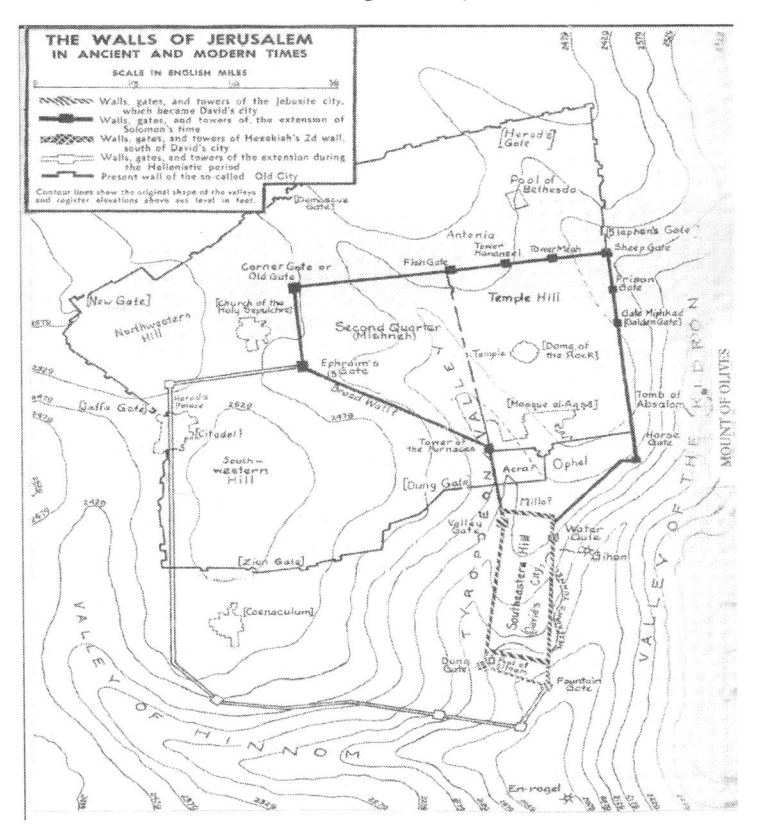

The Question

But because Jesus did not elaborate as to when the destruction of the Temple and the city of Jerusalem were going to take place, after Jesus settled on Mount Olives that Wednesday evening, and many of His followers had left His presence that night, the disciples came to Jesus and said to Him, "7 when shall these things be? and what **sign** will there be when these things shall come to pass?" (Luke 21:7).

In response, regarding to the "sign," which would reveal that the destruction of Jerusalem was at hand, Jesus said to the apostles,

> "15 When ye [all of you] therefore shall see the abomination of desolation, spoken of by Daniel the prophet, stand in the holy place, (whoso readeth, let him understand)" (Matthew 24:15).

And when the people in Jerusalem and in Judaea "see the abomination of desolation, spoken of by Daniel the prophet, stand in the holy place," they were to "16 flee into the mountains:" and Jesus added, "17 Let him which is on the housetop not come down to take any thing out of his house: 18 Neither let him which is in the field return back to take his clothes. 19 And woe unto them that are with child, and to them that give suck in those days! 20 But pray ye that your flight be not in the winter, neither on the Sabbath [Saturday] day:" Matthew 24:16-20

Surprised at the revelation of the "sign" and of the events that would lead to the destruction of the city and of the Temple; the disciples were quite uneasy with their thoughts

The Question

that night.

The next day, Thursday 13, 31 AD, Jesus had His disciples prepare for the Passover meal (Matthew 26:17-19). And after the sun went down, that Thursday night, "He sat down with the twelve" disciples to celebrate the Passover (Matthew 26:17). "2 And supper being ended…4 He riseth from supper, and laid aside His garments; and took a towel, and girded Himself" (John 13:2-4). In doing so, He performed the LORD'S Supper with humility. (See John 13:1-30; Matthew 26:21-25.)

After the LORD'S Supper ended and Judas was on his way to the priests to betray Christ, briefly here are some of the sequential events that followed: After Judas left the room, Jesus and the rest of the disciples went to the garden of Gethsemane where Jesus prayed and prepared for His betrayal to take place (Matthew 26:36-46). The betrayal by Judas (Matthew 26:47-56). Before Annas and then Caiaphas the high priest (a son-in-law of Annas), other priests, elders, and scribes (26:57-64). The Sanhedrin, at the trial, Caiaphas rent his clothes and passed the death sentence upon Christ the LORD on the charge of "blasphemy" (Matt. 26:65, 66). Then they mocked Him, ridiculed Him, spit on His face, hit Him, and as they hit Him, they asked Him mockingly, "Who hit You?" (Matthew 26:67-68; Luke 22:63-71); after that they prepared to take Christ to Pilate. And when Friday morning, the 14th rolled in, Caiaphas the high priest, the other priests, elders, and scribes, who were in a closed session, brought Christ to Pilate the Roman governor to execute Him (Matt. 27:1, 2).

Eventually and reluctantly, Pilate ordered Christ to be crucified. Here is the reference: "28 Then led they [the Jewish leaders] Jesus from Caiaphas unto the hall of judgment: and it was early [Friday morning]; and they [the Jewish leaders] themselves went not into the judgment hall, lest they should be defiled; but that they might eat the Passover:

The Question

"₂₉ Pilate then went out unto them, and said, What accusation bring ye [all of you] against this man?

"₃₀ They answered and said unto him, If He were not a malefactor, we would not have delivered Him up unto thee [you].

"₃₁ Then said Pilate unto them, Take ye [all of you] Him, and judge Him according to your law. The Jews therefore said unto him, It is not lawful for us to put any man to death: ₃₂ That the saying of Jesus might be fulfilled, which He spake, signifying what death He should die.

"₃₃ Then Pilate entered into the judgment hall again, and called Jesus, and said unto Him, Art Thou [You] the King of the Jews? ₃₄ Jesus answered him, Sayest thou [you] this thing of thyself [yourself], or did others tell it thee [you] of Me?

"₃₅ Pilate answered, Am I a Jew? Thine [Your] own nation and the chief priests have delivered Thee [You] unto me: what hast Thou [You] done? ₃₆ Jesus answered, My kingdom is not of this world: if my kingdom were of this world, then would My servants fight, that I should not be delivered to the Jews: but now is My kingdom not from hence. ₃₇ Pilate therefore said unto him, Art Thou [You] a king then? Jesus answered, Thou [you] sayest that I am a king. To this end was I born, and for this cause came I into the world, that I should bear witness unto the truth. Every one that is of the truth heareth my voice.

"₃₈ Pilate saith unto Him, What is truth? And when he had said this, he went out again unto the Jews, and saith unto them, I find in Him no fault at all. ₃₉ But ye have a custom, that

The Question

I should release unto you one at the passover: will ye [all of you] therefore that I release unto you the King of the Jews?

> "40 Then cried they all again, saying, Not this man, but Barabbas. Now Barabbas was a robber."

> "1 Then Pilate therefore took Jesus, and scourged Him. 2 And the soldiers platted a crown of thorns, and put it on His head, and they put on Him a purple robe, 3 And said, Hail, King of the Jews! and they smote Him with their hands.

> "4 Pilate therefore went forth again, and saith unto them, Behold, I bring Him forth to you, that ye [all of you] may know that I find no fault in Him.

> "5 Then came Jesus forth, wearing the crown of thorns, and the purple robe. And Pilate saith unto them, Behold the Man! 6 When the chief priests therefore and officers saw Him, they cried out, saying, Crucify Him, crucify Him. Pilate saith unto them, Take ye [all of you] Him, and crucify Him: for I find no fault in Him.

> "7 The Jews answered him, We have a law, and by our law He ought to die, because He made Himself the Son of God.

> "8 When Pilate therefore heard that saying, he was the more afraid; 9 And went again into the judgment hall, and saith unto Jesus, Whence art Thou [You]? But Jesus gave him no answer.

> "10 Then saith Pilate unto him, Speakest Thou [You] not unto me? knowest Thou [You] not that I have power to crucify Thee [You], and have power to release Thee [You]?

>> "11 Jesus answered, Thou [you] couldest have no power at all against Me, except it were given thee [you] from above: therefore he that delivered Me unto thee [you] hath the greater sin.

The Question

"₁₂ And from thenceforth Pilate sought to release Him: but the Jews cried out, saying, If thou let this Man go, thou [you] art not Caesar's friend: whosoever maketh himself a king speaketh against Caesar.

"₁₃ When Pilate therefore heard that saying, he brought Jesus forth, and sat down in the judgment seat in a place that is called the Pavement, but in the Hebrew, Gabbatha. ₁₄ And it was the preparation of the passover, and about the sixth hour: and he saith unto the Jews, Behold your King!

"₁₅ But they cried out, Away with Him, away with Him, crucify Him.

"Pilate saith unto them, Shall I crucify your King?

"The chief priests answered, We have no king but Caesar.

"₁₆ Then delivered he Him therefore unto them to be crucified. And they took Jesus, and led Him away. ₁₇ And He bearing His cross went forth into a place called the place of a skull, which is called in the Hebrew Golgotha:

"₁₈ Where they crucified Him, and two other with Him, on either side one, and Jesus in the midst.

"₁₉ And Pilate wrote a title, and put it on the cross. And the writing was, JESUS OF NAZARETH THE KING OF THE JEWS.

"₂₀ This title then read many of the Jews: for the place where Jesus was crucified was nigh to the city: and it was written in Hebrew, and Greek, and Latin.

"₂₁ Then said the chief priests of the Jews to Pilate, Write not, The King of the Jews; but that He said, I am King of the Jews.

"₂₂ Pilate answered, What I have written I have written.

The Question

"₂₃ Then the soldiers, when they had crucified Jesus, took His garments, and made four parts, to every soldier a part; and also His coat: now the coat was without seam, woven from the top throughout. ₂₄ They said therefore among themselves, Let us not rend it, but cast lots for it, whose it shall be: that the scripture might be fulfilled, which saith, They parted My raiment among them, and for My vesture they did cast lots. These things therefore the soldiers did.

"₂₅ Now there stood by the cross of Jesus His mother, and His mother's sister, Mary the wife of Cleophas, and Mary Magdalene.

"₂₆ When Jesus therefore saw His mother, and the disciple standing by, whom He loved, He saith unto His mother, Woman, behold thy [your] son! ₂₇ Then saith He to the disciple, Behold thy [your] mother! And from that hour that disciple took her unto his own home.

> "₂₈ After this, Jesus knowing that all things were now accomplished, that the scripture might be fulfilled, saith, I thirst.
>
> "₂₉ Now there was set a vessel full of vinegar: and they filled a sponge with vinegar, and put it upon hyssop, and put it to His mouth.
>
> "₃₀ When Jesus therefore had received the vinegar, He said, It is finished: and He bowed His head, and gave up the ghost.

"₃₁ The Jews therefore, because it was the preparation, that the bodies should not remain upon the cross on the sabbath day, (for that sabbath day was an high day,) besought Pilate that their legs might be broken, and that they might be taken away. ₃₂ Then came the soldiers, and brake the legs of the

The Question

first, and of the other which was crucified with Him. 33 But when they came to Jesus, and saw that He was dead already, they brake not His legs:

"34 But one of the soldiers with a spear pierced His side, and forthwith came there out blood and water.

"35 And he that saw it bare record, and his record is true: and he knoweth that he saith true, that ye might believe.

> "36 For these things were done, that the scripture should be fulfilled, A bone of Him shall not be broken.

"37 And again another scripture saith, They shall look on Him Whom they pierced." John 18:28-40; 19:1-37

"62 Now the next day, that followed the day of the preparation, the chief priests and Pharisees came together unto Pilate, 63 Saying, Sir, we remember that that deceiver said, while He was yet alive, After three days I will rise again. 64 Command therefore that the sepulchre be made sure until the third day, lest His disciples come by night, and steal Him away, and say unto the people, He is risen from the dead: so the last error shall be worse than the first.

"65 Pilate said unto them, Ye [all of you] have a watch: go your way, make it as sure as ye can.

"66 So they went, and made the sepulchre sure, sealing the stone, and setting a watch." Matthew 27:62-66.

"1 In the end of the Sabbath [Saturday], as it began to dawn toward the first day [Sunday] of the week, came Mary Magdalene and the other Mary to see the sepulchre. 2 And, behold, there was a great earthquake: for the angel of the Lord descended from heaven, and came and rolled back the stone from the door, and sat upon it. 3 His countenance was like lightning, and his raiment white as snow: 4 And for fear of him the keepers did shake, and became as dead men. 5 And the

The Question

angel answered and said unto the women, Fear not ye [all of you]: for I know that ye seek Jesus, which was crucified.

> "6 He is not here: for He is risen, as he said, Come, see the place where the LORD lay. 7 And go quickly, and tell His disciples that He is risen from the dead; and, behold, He goeth before you into Galilee; there shall ye see Him: lo, I have told you" (Matthew 28:1-7).

When the women saw the grave empty, they were overjoyed, and quickly sought information as to where all of the apostles were hiding from the Jews, in order to tell them that Jesus had risen; and to tell them what the angels said to them. After speaking to few of the disciples, they began to seek out the rest of the apostles to tell them that the LORD was going to meet with them in Galilee.

Shortly after His resurrection, Jesus came back from heaven and appeared to some of His disciples; and helped them to understand the Scripture, starting from Moses' writings. After giving the apostles understanding (Luke 24:22-31), the apostles met in unison; and when they were empowered by God the Holy Spirit, they became effective Gospel workers for Christ the LORD of hosts. They went everywhere healing in the name of Jesus and preaching Jesus Christ crucified and Christ risen from the dead.

And, on their travels in Judaea, the apostles also warned and preached that Jerusalem would be destroyed. And in order for the dwellers of Jerusalem not to suffer abuse, starvation, disease, and perish in the destruction of the city, the apostles revealed the events to the dwellers of Judah, but more in particular to the people who lived in Jerusalem, and the "sign" that would tell them to flee immediately from Jerusalem. When they see the "sign," they were to drop whatever they

The Question

were doing right on the spot and run to the mountains and hide.

Most of the Jews, instead of thanking the apostles for the warning and for the Gospel message, they followed them, persecuted them, blasphemed them, and defamed their character before the crowds. But, Christ the LORD would not allow the Jews or anybody else to hinder or suppress the Gospel message; it was to go to the world as a witness against those who despise it. But, the Sanhedrin had its people stir the crowds against the apostles. Finally, at one point, "46 Paul and Barnabas waxed bold, and said [to the Jews],

> "It was necessary that the word of God should first have been spoken to you: but seeing ye [all of you] put it from you, and judge yourselves unworthy of everlasting life, lo, we turn to the Gentiles." Acts 13:46

In doing so, they began to turn the world upside down with their message. But it was not easy; they still met persecution, starvation, beatings, jail, shipwreck, and even death, all because they were fervently preaching Jesus Christ's death and resurrection for the sins of the world. And that kind of preaching was not welcomed, especially in Jerusalem, by the majority of the Jewish people, and, by their pagan King Agrippa. They killed Apostle James the son of Zebedee – the brother of Apostle John; and imprisoned Apostle Peter. (See Matt. 4:21; Acts 12:1-7.)

Although the apostles and those who identified themselves as Christians were persecuted, there were many Jews who secretly accepted Christ as their personal LORD God and Savior, believed the Gospel message, and that Jerusalem was going to be destroyed. Therefore they watched diligently for the "sign" so that they and their families would be

The Question

able to flee the city in time.

So! What was the "sign" that they were to watch for? According to Apostle Luke, the answer is

"20 when ye [all of you] shall see Jerusalem compassed with armies," (Luke 21:20).

And Jesus added, "20 then know that the desolation thereof is nigh [near]" (Luke 21:20). In other words, when you see Jerusalem surrounded "with armies," then know that the destruction of Jerusalem was "near."
Of what armies is Apostle Luke talking about?

The answer is given?
Luke writes that it is the armies of "the Gentiles."
Here is the reference:

"24 And they shall fall by the edge of the sword, and shall be led away captive into all nations: and Jerusalem shall be trodden down of the Gentiles, until the times of the Gentiles be fulfilled." Luke 21:24

And the next question that rises from the above statement is to ask, what Gentile army was going to destroy the beautiful buildings of Jerusalem and its Sanctuary to the ground?
Historically, it was the contemporary Roman pagan army of Caesar that destroyed Jerusalem to the ground, in 70 AD of which Jesus predicted.
But, before the city of Jerusalem was destroyed, by the savage Roman army, the first siege around Jerusalem remained inactive for quite some time. And the reason the Roman army

The Question

did not invade Jerusalem at that time was due to the fact that Vespasian, a Roman general, who was ordered by Caesar to remove and suppress all of the insurgence from Palestine — more precisely the Jewish insurgence and their leaders in Jerusalem — did not attack the city because word came that Nero was dead. Vespasian was close to striking Jerusalem, but the news that Nero was dead sidetracked Vespasian's thinking. In response to Nero's death, Vespasian encouraged by his army became self appointed Emperor of the Roman Empire, by first removing those who wanted to occupy Caesar's seat. Once that task was accomplished, Vespasian moved to Rome to rule his empire.

Emperor Vespasian ruled from Rome for ten years (69-79 AD).

But before Vespasian went to Rome to take the mighty coveted grand seat of Caesar, he gave the mission and the army, which he commanded, to his trusted son Titus to go forward and eradicate all of the uprisings, and that included those that were in the city of Jerusalem. And that transfer of power to Titus by his father Vespasian, which postponed the siege of Jerusalem, was the "sign" Jesus was talking about in Luke 21:20.

Jesus said,

> "[20] And when ye [all of you] shall see Jerusalem compassed with armies, then know that the desolation thereof is nigh" Luke 21:20

And then, Jesus forewarned as to what was going to transpire, and, when the siege of Jerusalem was to take place. He said,

> "[21] Then" (when "Jerusalem compassed with armies"), "let them which are in Judaea flee to

The Question

the mountains; and let them which are in the midst of it depart out; and let not them that are in the countries enter thereinto. 22 For these be the days of vengeance, that all things which are written may be fulfilled.

"23 But woe unto them that are with child, and to them that give suck, in those days! for there shall be great distress in the land, and wrath upon this people. 24 And they shall fall by the edge of the sword, and shall be led away captive into all nations: and Jerusalem shall be trodden down of the Gentiles, until the times of the Gentiles be fulfilled." Luke 21:21-24

The "sign" then, which would reveal that the siege and the destruction of Jerusalem was eminent is clearly revealed in Luke 21:20-24

Please note; Jesus was talking about a "sign," He was not talking about signs. There was one "sign," and as you have read, it is described as follows

"20 And when ye [all of you] shall see Jerusalem compassed with armies, then know that the desolation thereof is nigh" (Luke 21:20).

And once the people in Jerusalem saw Jerusalem encircled by "armies," they were to leave immediately. Jesus said,

"21 Then, let them which are in Judaea flee to the mountains; and let them which are in the midst of it depart out; and let not them that are in the countries enter thereinto." Luke 21:21

The Question

If they did not want to perish in the city by the Roman sword, they were to drop what they were doing and flee the city right away.

Although the warning was given over and over to the citizens of Jerusalem, needless to say at this point, those individuals who did not believe Christ's words did not leave Jerusalem. But, in their predicament, whished that they had left when the Roman soldiers who encamped Jerusalem the first time pulled back their forces and did not stop anyone from leaving the city. But now, in the spring of 70 AD, the siege upon Jerusalem had come. Titus weighed his options. And to give Titus a good view of the city, Titus settled on Mount Olives and encircled the city. He wanted the leaders of the insurgence to surrender, instead, they refused. And that refusal unleashed the deadly Roman siege. And to make matters even worse, those hotheaded insurgents, which were within the city fought amongst themselves for supremacy while the siege of Jerusalem was taking place at the outer wall of the city. And while the bickering amongst the Jewish insurgence continued, the forces of Titus captured the outer wall of Jerusalem in May of 70 AD sealing the destination of all that were in the city. Unfortunately, at that time, there were thousands upon thousands of visitors who had came to Jerusalem to celebrate the Passover and stayed little bit longer in the city. Their stay created shortage of food and water and accommodations sooner than they anticipated.

While the siege continued, the leaders in Jerusalem thought that the God of their forefathers was on their side; and therefore they advised the Jerusalemites not to give up hope. They were to fight on. But, when the Roman army broke through the first wall of Jerusalem, in their zealot efforts, the Jews were killed by the thousands. In fact, in the three months period, May to July, there were over one hundred thousand Jews killed by disease and starvation. And those individuals

The Question

who escaped death and were captured by the Roman army, Titus crucified on the hills of Judaea.

Once the armed forces of Titus broke through the second wall of Jerusalem, the destruction of human life, buildings, property, silver, gold, etc., etc., became free for all. The city was looted and torched and leveled to the ground, as it was predicted by Jesus Christ the LORD. By the end of August 70 AD, the army was victorious over Jerusalem. And, if victory was not enough for Titus, it has been estimated that the Romans took ninety-seven thousand prisoners to sell, enslave, or to use them in their arenas for sport.

Although the city of Jerusalem was secured by Titus' Roman army, the brutal fighting continued throughout Judaea for three more years in order to remove all of the insurgence from the land. The insurgents were killed, sold, or enslaved as the army swept across the land. The Romans conquered village after village, town after town, fortress after fortress, and by May of 73 AD, the bloody inhumane war between the Jews and Rome was over.

The merciless savagery of the onslaught, which marked the siege and capture of Jerusalem was perhaps the worst emotional Jewish wars because at the end, they lost the city and the Temple and a warning as to what would happen if another uprising took place. The Jews fought needlessly one another internally, and the Jews fought the Romans with the courage of desperation, and with hope of divine deliverance. On the other hand, the Romans captured and sold the Jews into slavery, and sent others for sport by the thousands to various cities throughout the world to perish in the arenas. It did not have to be that way; if only the Jewish leaders and their followers would have listened to Christ's words and left the city – with those that did – when the "sign" appeared before their eyes.

Although the Roman army and Roman citizens occupied Jerusalem in 70 AD and lived with a smaller number

The Question

of Jews in the city, when were "the times of the Gentiles be fulfilled"? Luke 21:24

Although the Romans demolished the activities of the Jewish system that evolved around the Temple (Sanctuary), which was in Jerusalem, now with the Temple destroyed, and all means of the Sanhedrin self-government dispersed, the Jews tried to restructure their lives around the Law of Moses in their synagogues. But, that effort did not meet and it has not met the requirements of the law, even today. The ceremonial law requires a sinner to offer and sacrifice an animal in the eastern courtyard of the Sanctuary, which is in Jerusalem, for the sins of the penitent sinner. For the past 2,000 years, this requirement has not been implemented for the sinners by the Levite priests in the eastern courtyard of the Sanctuary; so how were and how are the penitent sinners forgiven and saved from their sins without the remission of the blood of the animals in the eastern courtyard of the Sanctuary?

A good question don't you think? And one that should be given a great deal of consideration.

Nonetheless, although the Jews were defeated in 70 AD, they did not learn the lesson that Rome was serious about the Jewish behavior. They were becoming a thorn in their side because the Jewish insurgence started all over again in 132 AD. Only this time, the Roman army was told to eradicate the Jews from Palestine. And in regards to the city of Jerusalem, the Roman army not only captured the city for the second time, but also made a decree that no Jew was to enter Jerusalem again; if they did, they were to be executed for trespassing. By the removal of all Jews from the city, Jerusalem became a city of the Gentiles.

Consequently, in the Temple area, the Roman authorities erected a temple to Jupiter their god; and in 135 AD, Jerusalem became the "Capitol of the Gentiles." Thus fulfilling the words of Jesus when He said,

The Sign in Matthew 24 By: Philip Mitanidis
The Question

> "24 Jerusalem shall be trodden down of the Gentiles, until the times of the Gentiles be fulfilled." Luke 21:20-24

The time of the Gentiles were fulfilled in 135 AD. The Romans occupied Jerusalem, set up their gods in the city and outside of the city. And, as far as the Jews were concerned, they lost Jerusalem, the Temple, Palestine, and roamed the earth for 2,000 years. The Jews became a byword and a people without a country; all because they would not take heed to the words of Christ the LORD God of Abraham when He forewarned Solomon and those that followed:

> *The admonition*: "3 And the LORD said unto him, I have heard thy [your] prayer and thy [your] supplication, that thou [you] hast made before Me: I have hallowed this house, which thou [you] hast built, to put My name there for ever; and Mine eyes and Mine heart shall be there perpetually. 4 And if thou [you] wilt walk before me, as David thy [your] father walked, in integrity of heart, and in uprightness, to do according to all that I have commanded thee [you], and wilt keep My statutes and My judgments: 5 Then I will establish the throne of thy [your] kingdom upon Israel for ever, as I promised to David thy [your] father, saying, There shall not fail thee [you] a man upon the throne of Israel.

> *The Warning*: "6 But if ye [all of you] shall at all turn from following Me, ye [all of you] or your children, and will not keep My commandments and My statutes which I have set before

The Question

you, but go and serve other gods, and worship them:

"7 Then will I cut off Israel out of the land which I have given them; and this house [the Sanctuary], which I have hallowed for My name, will I cast out of My sight; and Israel shall be a proverb and a byword among all people:

"8 And at this house, which is high, every one that passeth by it shall be astonished, and shall hiss; and they shall say, Why hath the LORD done thus unto this land, and to this house?

"9 And they shall answer, Because they forsook the LORD their God, who brought forth their fathers out of the land of Egypt, and have taken hold upon other gods, and have worshipped them, and served them: therefore hath the LORD brought upon them all this evil." 1 Kings 9:3-9

Finally, Daniel's words (Daniel 9:27), which were written about 600 years before Christ came in the flesh, and Christ's words, which were spoken in 31 AD were fulfilled by the Roman armies. The Roman's destroyed Jerusalem in 70 AD; and in 135 AD, they were,

"14 standing [in Jerusalem's holy Temple area] where it ought not" (Mark 13:14).

They rebuilt Jerusalem; and a temple to Jupiter was erected by the Roman authorities on the area where the

The Question

Temple of Solomon once stood. And to irk the Jews to no end, Jerusalem was renamed as the "Capitol of the Gentiles." Jerusalem became a Gentile city; governed by the Roman outstretched arm. And to avoid another uprising by the Jews, a law was enacted in 135 AD, which stated that no Jews were allowed to enter the city of Jerusalem. If they did, the intruders would face – by law – the penalty of torture, pain, and death.

And the rest of the story, you probably already know that the Jews as a nation were terminated and were dispersed throughout the world until 1948 when England allowed them to return to Jerusalem; and even then, the Sanctuary (Temple) is still inactive and split by the English into two parts. The "most holy" place of the Sanctuary was given to the Muslims; and the "holy place" of the Sanctuary was given to the Jews. And this division has caused negotiations between the Muslims and Jews to disagree because the Muslims want all of the Sanctuary for their god, and the Jews want all of the Sanctuary for their god; and that desire irks both sides to no end.

Paradoxically, the Muslims and the Jews reject Jesus Christ the LORD God of Abraham as their LORD God and Savior (John 1:11). And, according to the inspired Scripture (Bible), since they cannot go directly to God the Father to worship him and be saved (John 14:6), unto what god are they prepared to give the dilapidated, dormant, and padlocked Sanctuary to? And, will the Gentiles allow them to do it?

If not, Israel shall remain,

"7 a proverb and a byword among all people:

"8 And at this house [the Sanctuary], which is high, every one that passeth by it shall be astonished, and shall hiss; and they shall say, Why hath the LORD done thus unto this land, and to this house?

The Question

"9 And they shall answer, Because they forsook the LORD their God [Christ], who brought forth their fathers out of the land of Egypt, and have taken hold upon other gods, and have worshipped them, and served them: therefore hath the LORD brought upon them all this evil." 1 Kings 9:7-9

~~~

The Second Question

After Jesus settled on Mount Olives that Wednesday evening in April 12, 31 AD, and many of His followers had left His presence that night, as you have read in the previous chapter, Jesus did reveal and describe to His disciples the "sign" that was going to take place before Jerusalem fell into a devastating destruction.

But that was not the only "sign" the disciples were inquiring about. They also wanted to know what was the "sign," which would reveal that Christ's second coming was around the corner?

If you recall, four of His disciples, James, John, Peter, and Andrew went privately to Christ that night and said to Him,

> "3 Tell us, when shall these things be? and what shall be the **sign** of Thy [Your] coming, and of the end of the world?" Matthew 24:3

As you have read in the above verse, the apostles did not mix words; they were straightforward with their questions. They wanted to know,

1) "what shall be the sign of Thy [Your] coming, and
2) "the end of the world?"

So, "what shall be the sign," or what does the "sign" look like?

Surprisingly, Jesus did not answer their request, at that time. But, at the same time, Jesus did specify that a "sign"

The Second Question

would appear for all to see before He comes the second time.

Although Christ mentioned a "sign" to the apostles, it appears from the four Gospel writers, the "sign" was not revealed or described to them. And yet, Jesus did speak to them of a "sign"! And that "sign," which is not revealed in the four Gospels, was to appear as a warning to the entire world that Christ's second coming is at hand. The point was well taken that the "sign" would remain aloof until Jesus Christ decides when to reveal it and describe it. But for now, the apostles accepted the brief overview of what would happen before the "sign" is revealed to the entire world; and what would happen before Christ comes the second time.

But, if people do not know what the "sign" looks like, even if they were to see it, how are they to know if it is the "sign," which reveals that the second coming of Christ is at hand?

The above presentation might appear inconsistent; but, do you really think that Christ would go to such lengths to mention that a "sign" will appear to indicate that Christ's second coming is near, and not describe it for us?

Of course He will describe it for us; otherwise why bother mentioning it?

But, before Jesus describes the "sign" for us, as in the previous chapter, Jesus was more concerned about His disciple's well being; and therefore, He began to describe, in a brief overview, the events that would effect them before the "sign" appears for all the world to see.

Here is the overview with my comments, from Matthew chapter twenty-four; it reads as follows:

> "4 And Jesus answered and said unto them [the disciples], Take heed that no man deceive you. 5 For many shall come in My name, saying, I am Christ; and shall deceive many. 6 And ye [all

The Second Question

of you] shall hear of wars and rumours of wars: see that ye be not troubled: for all these things must come to pass, but the end is not yet."

In the above verses, Jesus is revealing to the disciples the events that would take place during their lifetime; and the following verses reveal the events that would take place after their lifetime. Jesus said to them;

"7 For nation shall rise against nation, and kingdom against kingdom: and there shall be famines, and pestilences, and earthquakes, in divers places. 8 All these are the beginning of sorrows." Matthew 24:4-8 (See also Mark 13:5-8; Luke 21:5-11.)

Verse seven, above, refers to the time period after the Roman Empire fragmented in 467 AD. It refers to that time period because the verse says, "7 For nation shall rise against nation, and kingdom against kingdom: and there shall be famines, and pestilences, and earthquakes, in divers places."

It should be noted that there were no "nations rising against nations" or "kingdoms rising against kingdoms" during the 644 years of iron rule by the Roman Empire. There were partisans and insurgence and trouble spots in the Roman Empire from 168 BC to 476 AD, as you have read in the first chapter, which were quelled, but there were no "nations" or "kingdoms" fighting against each other as they did after the Roman Empire fell, and are still fighting today. Therefore the time period of verses seven and eight apply to the time period after the Roman Empire fragmented.

And verse eight, which is self explanatory, in reference to the above events, says, "8 All these are the beginning of sorrows."

The Second Question

And verse nine says, "9 Then shall they deliver you up to be afflicted, and shall kill you: and ye [all of you] shall be hated of all nations for My name's sake." Matthew 24:8, 9

In order to clarify verse nine, let me take you to the parallel statement of Apostle Luke, which reads;

> "12 But before all these, they shall lay their hands on you, and persecute you, delivering you up to the synagogues, and into prisons, being brought before kings and rulers for My name's sake." Luke 21:12

Did you notice?

In reference to verses seven and eight of Matthew twenty-four, Luke says, "before all these," things that are mentioned in Matthew 24:7, 8, and Luke 21:10, 11, "9 Then shall they deliver you up to be afflicted, and shall kill you: and ye [all of you] shall be hated of all nations for My name's sake." Matthew 24:9

But, "before all these" events of Matthew 24:7, 8, and Luke 21:10, 11, the apostles were going to be persecuted and even some of them killed.

So, why were the apostles "afflicted" and "killed" and "hated" of all nations? They were because they went into countries, which possessed and worshipped pagan gods that despised Jesus Christ and His disciples for preaching His Gospel message in His name. And that created animosity by the pagan worshippers upon those who converted to Christianity; and upon the disciples for helping them to convert to Jesus Christ.

We are told;

> "10 And then shall many be offended, and shall betray one another, and shall hate one

The Second Question

> another. 11 And many false prophets shall rise, and shall deceive many. 12 And because iniquity shall abound, the love of many shall wax cold. 13 But he that shall endure unto the end, the same shall be saved." Matthew 24:10-13

After giving a brief overview to the apostles, starting from their time period, 31 AD, all the way down to our time period when "7 nation shall rise against nation, and kingdom against kingdom: and there shall be famines, and pestilences, and earthquakes, in divers places." "8 All these are the beginning of sorrows" (Matthew 24:7, 8); Jesus redirects their thinking to the events that would take place in regards to Jerusalem and its outcome. (See Mathew 24:15-20.)

And after Jesus finished talking about Jerusalem and its outcome, Jesus went back to the subject of the "sign" and of His 2nd coming.

And in regards to our time period (Matthew 24:7, 8), who can deny all of the wars and rumors of wars and nation rising against another nation and kingdom rising against another kingdom? And who can deny the mega weather patterns planet earth is experiencing? And who can deny the cataclysmic typhoons, flooding, famines, earthquakes, pestilence, uncontrollable fires, tornados, hurricanes, mud slides, sink holes, massive smog formations, poverty, slavery, deadly genetic modified foods, gluten in your food and drinks, prison camps, forced laws, immorality, massive unemployment, etc., etc., we are experiencing today? (See 2 Timothy 3:1-7, 13,)

Were not "8 All these" "the beginning of sorrows" for the apostles up until the fall of Jerusalem in 135 AD? And were not "8 All these" "the beginning of sorrows," for the Gentiles and Christians right after the fall of Jerusalem in 135 AD?

Obviously they were!

But, how far down the prophetic corridors of time was

The Second Question

Jesus referring to before the "sign" would appear? Here is one of His clues.

> "₁₄ And this gospel of the kingdom shall be preached in all the world for a witness unto all nations; and then shall the end come." Matthew 24:14

Did you notice? Jesus said, "**this** Gospel" shall be preached before the "end comes." Jesus is referring to His Gospel (Mark 1:1), the Gospel He was preaching and the apostles were preaching and wrote about for us to read.

So! According to verse fourteen, Christ's Gospel will be preached just before the end of the world comes.

And who will preach the Gospel Jesus was preaching and the apostles were preaching to the world?

As per scripture, it is the three angels of Revelation chapter fourteen.

But, why were three angels commissioned to go and preach the everlasting Gospel of Jesus to the world? Are not the three humongous religious denominations, the Muslims, Jews, and Christians preaching the everlasting Gospel of Jesus Christ to the world?

Well, if they were or if even one of them is preaching the everlasting Gospel of Jesus Christ today, why are they all bypassed and the task of preaching the everlasting Gospel of Jesus Christ to the world is given to the three angels to accomplish?

It is given to the three angels to preach the everlasting Gospel of Jesus because these three humongous religious bodies are not preaching the Gospel of Jesus. True, each church denomination is preaching the Gospel of Jesus in part or to some degree, if you like; but they are not preaching the full Gospel of Jesus Christ. And that is the reason why the

The Second Question

three angels have been commissioned to go and find willing hands to preach the full Gospel message of Jesus to a perishing world.

~ ~ ~

> *The Three Angel's Messages:* "6 And I [Apostle John] saw another angel fly in the midst of heaven, having the everlasting gospel to preach unto them that dwell on the earth, and to every nation, and kindred, and tongue, and people, 7 Saying with a loud voice, Fear God, and give glory to Him; for the hour of His judgment is come: and worship Him [Christ] that made heaven, and earth, and the sea, and the fountains of waters.
>
> "8 And there followed another angel, saying, Babylon is fallen, is fallen, that great city, because she made all nations drink of the wine of the wrath of her fornication.
>
> "9 And the third angel followed them, saying with a loud voice, If any man worship the beast and his image, and receive [his] mark in his forehead, or in his hand, 10 The same shall drink of the wine of the wrath of God, which is poured out without mixture into the cup of his indignation; and he shall be tormented with fire and brimstone in the presence of the holy angels, and in the presence of the Lamb: 11 And the smoke of their torment ascendeth up for ever and ever: and they have no rest day nor night, who worship the beast and his image, and whosoever receiveth the mark of his name." Revelation 14:6-11

The First Angel's Message

The proclamation by the first angel: _____ According to verses six and seven, the first angel will proclaim three messages. They are,

> 1) -- "having the everlasting gospel to preach unto them that dwell on the earth."
> 2) -- "Fear God, and give glory to Him; for the hour of His judgment is come:"
> 3) -- "and worship Him [Christ] that made heaven, and earth, and the sea, and the fountains of waters."

1). *Having the everlasting gospel to preach:* _____ In point number one, it is obvious that the first angel has been commissioned to preach "the everlasting gospel" "unto them that dwell on the earth." And the other obvious point is the fact that the everlasting Gospel the first angel is commissioned to preach is the Gospel Jesus and the apostles were preaching.

So! By whom is the first angel going to preach the everlasting Gospel of Jesus Christ (Mark 1:1), before the end of the world takes place?

Obviously, it will be preached by willing human hands.

But, is the Gospel not preached today by the Christian churches or by the Muslim mosques or by the Jewish synagogues?

According to scripture, obviously not!

Consider the following two points.   a). Factually, all of

The First Angel's Message - ***everlasting gospel to preach***

these three humungous religions have multiple churches in their midst that do not agree with each other's doctrines. And on top of that, if you were to consider the diverse teachings within the Muslim faith, or the diverse teachings within the Jewish faith, or if you were to consider the diverse teachings within the Christian churches, you will find that they all do not agree with each other's doctrinal teachings. It has been estimated that there are over 12,500 doctrinal beliefs out there. And if you were to ask any one of them whose doctrine is right or true, each one of them will answer and say, "Our doctrine is the correct one, and the other doctrines are wrong." So! Since they all claim that their religious doctrines are correct, and since they all claim that the other's doctrinal beliefs are wrong; we can ask, who is preaching today the everlasting Gospel of Jesus Christ, if these three humongous denominations are not?

To answer, it is the first angel who is recruiting willing hands to go and preach Christ's Gospel to a perishing world.

And, if you were to consider point b), you will also find that all of these three diverse humongous religions, although they preach Jesus Christ in one degree or another, they fail to preach the Gospel doctrine. For example, the Muslims, Jews, and Christian denominations do not want to accept the fact that the writings of Moses and the rest of the Bible writers wrote about Jesus Christ the LORD of hosts (John 5:46, 47). They do not want to accept the fact that Jesus Christ is the LORD God of Abraham (Exodus 3:14, 15). And if you were to ask them to show you one verse from the Qur'an or from the Old Testament (Bible) where the prophet is referring to God the Father, the majority cannot do it. And, if you were to ask them who is the Creator of "all things," the majority will mislead you by saying, it is God the Father. And to make matters even worse, they take the Old Testament names that belong to Jesus Christ the LORD and brazenly apply them to God the Father, and so on go their opinionated beliefs.

The First Angel's Message - **everlasting gospel to preach:**

Therefore a person can conclude, since their religious doctrines are so far removed from the Gospel doctrine of Jesus Christ the LORD, and misrepresent Christ the LORD, it means that they are not preaching the Gospel Jesus Christ was preaching, or the Gospel the apostles were preaching. True, we can agree that they are preaching in one degree or another Jesus Christ; but they are not preaching His entire everlasting Gospel, which contains the everlasting Gospel doctrine. And since they are not preaching the everlasting Gospel doctrine they do not have Jesus Christ abiding with them; and neither do they have God the Father abiding with them. Here is the reason why?

We are told:

"9 Whosoever transgresseth, and abideth not in the doctrine of Christ, hath not God. He that abideth in the doctrine of Christ, he hath both the Father and the Son.

And then, the prophet of the LORD adds;

"10 If there come any unto you, and bring not this doctrine [the doctrine Jesus was preaching], receive him not into your house, neither bid him God speed:" 2 John 9, 10.

Very strong language don't you think?
See also Galatians 1:8

Consequently, since the three humongous religious institutions do not have the doctrine of Christ; it means also that they do not preach fully the everlasting Gospel of Jesus Christ. And because they are not preaching fully Christ's everlasting Gospel, Christ the LORD of hosts, in His mercy is reaching out to them by saying, "14 And unto the angel of the church of the Laodiceans write; These things saith the Amen

The First Angel's Message - **everlasting gospel to preach**

[Christ], the faithful and true witness, the beginning of the creation of God; 15 I know thy [your] works, that thou [you] art neither cold nor hot: I would thou [you] wert cold or hot. 16 So then because thou [you] art lukewarm, and neither cold nor hot, I will spue thee [you] out of my mouth.

> "17 Because thou [you] sayest, I am rich, and increased with goods, and have need of nothing; and knowest not that thou [you] art wretched, and miserable, and poor, and blind, and naked:
>
> "18 I counsel thee to buy of Me gold tried in the fire, that thou [you] mayest be rich; and white raiment, that thou mayest be clothed, and that the shame of thy nakedness do not appear; and anoint thine [your] eyes with eyesalve, that thou mayest see.
>
> "19 As many as I love, I rebuke and chasten: be zealous therefore, and repent.
>
> "20 Behold, I stand at the door, and knock: if any man hear my voice, and open the door, I will come in to him, and will sup with him, and he with Me. 21 To him that overcometh will I grant to sit with me in My throne, even as I also overcame, and am set down with my Father in his throne. 22 He that hath an ear, let him hear what the Spirit saith unto the churches." Revelation 3:14-22

As you probably already know, the Book of Revelation is compiled by the testimony of Jesus Christ the LORD of hosts (Revelation 1:2). Therefore the above presentation is the testimony of Jesus Christ (the Amen v.14) who is admonishing the last church (Laodiceans) to repent. The word Laodiceans refers to all of the churches, which use the Bible as their reference and claim that they are preaching the Gospel of Jesus Christ the LORD (v.19). Jesus says, all of these churches (Laodiceans) are "lukewarm." They are "neither cold nor hot." And because they are "neither cold nor hot," Jesus the Amen says that He is going to spue them out of His mouth" (v.16). Jesus also says to all of the churches that He knows their "works" (v.15) and describes their works. He says, "thou [you] art wretched, and miserable, and poor, and blind, and naked" (v.17). And therefore, He counsel's them to "18 buy of Me [Christ] gold tried in the fire, that thou [you] mayest be rich; and white raiment, that thou [you] mayest be clothed, and that the shame of thy [your] nakedness do not appear; and anoint thine [your] eyes with eyesalve, that thou [you] mayest see (v.18). And, if they would repent and overcome and do the will of Christ the LORD, He promises to each one of them by saying, "I [will] grant to sit with me in My throne" (v.21).

That is quite an offer to the repentant sinners.

Jesus promises them that they will sit on His throne, if they repent and do His will by preaching the everlasting Gospel and its doctrine to a perishing deceived world. But, if they choose not to, He says that He will spue them out of His mouth. In other words, He will reject them as His people.

2). *The Judgment is come:*_____ The second message that the first angel is commissioned to preach to a perishing world is to tell the world to,

> "7 Fear God, and give glory to Him; for the hour of His judgment is come:" Revelation 14:7

The First Angel's Message – **The Judgment is Come**

As you have noticed, in the above verse, the angel is saying, "His judgment is come."

So, why is he saying, "His judgment is come"?

He is saying that "His judgment is come" because all of those individuals who have died, ever since the fall of Adam and Eve, and claimed that they accepted Jesus Christ (the God of Israel) as their LORD God and Savior, they were judged first.

Here is the reference.

> "17 For the time is come that judgment must begin at the house of God: and if it first begin at us, what shall the end be of them that obey not the gospel of God?" 1 Peter 4:17

As per the above verse, judgment began first "at the house of God," meaning, the judgment began with those who call themselves Christians. It did not begin with the wicked. Therefore, judgment began first with Christ's dead saints, starting with Able. And after Christ's dead saints were judged, judgment came to the living saints. And now, since judgment has come to the living saints, the prophet of the LORD of hosts says, "judgment is come," and therefore, now, today, the living saints are being judged according to their acts. And this judgment will continue right up until the "sign" of Christ is revealed. But more accurately, right up to the time the decree is uttered (Revelation 22:11). At that time, people would have made up their minds whether to accept Christ as their personal Savior or not. At that time, after the last person on planet earth chooses Jesus Christ as his or her LORD God and Savior, God the Holy Spirit would not have any more people to bring to Jesus Christ the LORD to be saved. Therefore, probation for the human race would close, and Jesus Christ the LORD will at that time proclaim a decree, which states,

The First Angel's Message – **Worship Him**

> "₁₁ He that is unjust, let him be unjust still: and he which is filthy, let him be filthy still: and he that is righteous, let him be righteous still: and he that is holy, let him be holy still." Revelation 22:11

Once the above decree is proclaimed by Christ the LORD of hosts, there will be two classes of people on planet earth. One class will be wicked and the other class of people will be holy. And once that divide remains, Christ's penitent people who have gone through the "great tribulation" will be sealed by Christ's holy angels, and wait for Christ their Savior to come and take them to their heavenly home for 1,000 years. And after the 1,000 years expire, Christ, the holy angels, and the redeemed will return to the destroyed earth, and hover over the earth while all of the wicked dead on earth are resurrected. At that time every knee (Satan, evil angels, evil men, and evil women) on earth will bow before Christ the LORD of hosts (Philippians 2:10, 11), and then judgment will fall upon all of the wicked; and their reward will be given to them at that time according to their works.

3). *Worship Him that made heaven, and earth:* _____ The third message that the first angel is commissioned to preach to a perishing misguided world, by willing hands with the power of God the Holy Spirit, and in the name of Jesus is to tell the world to,

> "₇ worship Him [Christ] that made heaven, and earth, and the sea, and the fountains of waters." Revelation 14:7

Needless to say at this point and contrary to the above verse, it is common knowledge that the three humongous religious institutions (Muslim, Jewish, and Christian) believe

The First Angel's Message – **Worship Him**

and teach that it was God the Father, as we know him in the New Testament, who Created "all things." On the other side, you would find that the majority of the Christian churches disagree with their counterparts; they preach and teach people that God the Father has created "all things" "through" Jesus Christ. And the main reason why they believe as they do is the fact that they believe that the Old Testament creation verses refer to God the Father. But, if we apply the Old Testament creation verses to God the Father, those creation verses will tell us that there was no co-creator involved with God the Father. If there was no co-creator involved with God the Father, that means God the Father is the sole creator and Jesus Christ did not create a single thing because creation verses like Isaiah 44:24, if we apply them to God the Father, tell us that he created "all thing" "alone," and as he says, "by Myself." Isaiah 44:24

And to make matters even worse, if we go down that direction, we will make the New Testament creation verses to contradict the Old Testament creation verses because the New Testament Creation verses, in most mistranslated Bible translations, state that somebody created "through" Jesus Christ the LORD of hosts.

Now what?

Who is right?

And we can even go further and ask, are Scriptures contradicting each other? Or are the Muslims, Jews, and Christians that are contradicting the Scriptures? Or are the Bible translators that are contradicting the Scriptures?

To clear all of the misconceptions and contradictions regarding the Creator of the Bible, I have taken few pages from the supplement section of my book called "Moses Wrote About Me" BEEHIVE PUBLISHING HOUSE INC. 2013. pp 247-257. And while you are reading those few pages, under the title "Unwarranted Objections," please notice the Hebrew and the

The First Angel's Message – **Unwarranted Objections**

Greek texts; they all state the same thing, in the Old and New Testaments that there is only one Creator and that Creator is Jesus Christ the LORD of hosts better known by the prophets of old as the LORD God of Abraham.

Here is the supplement:

Unwarranted Objections

The Creator of the universe said to Jeremiah,

"4 command them [the delegates, who came to Jerusalem] to say unto their masters, thus saith the LORD of hosts, the God of Israel; Thus shall ye [all of you] say unto your masters;

"5 I have made the earth, the man and the beast that are upon the ground, by My great power and by My outstretched arm, and have given it unto whom it seemed meet unto Me." Jeremiah 27:4, 5

You know, a person would think, given that Christ acknowledges that He is "the LORD of hosts" and "the God of Israel" (v.4), and says by the mouth of Jeremiah, "5 I have made the earth, the man and the beast that are upon the ground, by My great power and by My outstretched arm" (Jeremiah 27:5), it should suffice for a person to acknowledge that Christ is the sole Creator; but, some people still disagree

The First Angel's Message – **_Unwarranted Objections_**

with the above Scripture references and with the previous chapter and state contrary to Scripture that there was a co-creator involved with the creation of the universe.

So, why are people insisting that there was a co-creator involved in the creation of "all things" when the above verses and in the previous chapters, the verses state so aptly that there is only one Creator who created "all things" "alone"?

Generally, they base their belief on three suppositions.

1). They believe that the Creator is God the Father.
2). On Genesis 1:26
3). On mistranslated Bible verses in the New Testament. I say in the New Testament because the Old Testament creation verses have been translated correctly. They do not contradict each other as the New Testament verses do in many Bible translations.

Nonetheless, let us consider their first objection.

1)_____ Although the objectors claim that it was God the Father who created the heavens and the earth; when asked to produce one single verse, which states that God the Father is the Creator, it cannot be done because there is no such verse or verses that can be produced from anywhere in the entire Bible.

All the objectors can do is to produce the creation verses, which refer to Christ the LORD of hosts, and then say that these verses refer to God the Father. Other than that, there is not a single reference to God the Father where it states that he is the Creator. The Scriptures are silent on that point.

The reason the objectors assume that the creation verses of the Old Testament refer to God the Father is due to the fact that they have been brought up to believe that way and not as a fact of Scripture; and therefore they claim and base their belief

The First Angel's Message – **Unwarranted Objections**

that God the Father is referred to, throughout the Old Testament, by the prophets of old. And that belief as per Scripture is one hundred percent in error.

Therefore, if I ask you to find one verse in the Old Testament where the prophets are referring to God the Father, as the God of Abraham and as the Creator, would you be able to produce one single verse? If you are unable to find one single verse, which refers to God the Father, as the God of Abraham and Creator of the universe, why would you believe that the Old Testament writers are writing about God the Father?

You know Christ the LORD of hosts personally stated to the house of Judah, particularly to the leaders of the house of Judah that the Scriptures testify of Him and not of God the Father. Christ said to His tempters:

> "39 Search the scriptures; for in them ye [all of you] think ye have eternal life; and they are they which testify of Me." John 5:39

How much plainer can Christ's statement be?

He said that the Old Testament Scriptures "testify of Me" and not about someone else. Christ the LORD of hosts referred to the Old Testament Scriptures because the New Testament Scriptures were not yet written.

Furthermore, Christ the LORD of hosts stated that the Torah (five books of Moses) testify of Him and not about His Associate (God the Father.) (I have used the word "Associate" throughout this book to refer to God the Father because God the Father did not become, God the Father until after Christ the LORD of hosts was born in the "flesh." Nonetheless Christ said to His tempters: "45 Do not think that I will accuse you to the Father: there is one that accuseth you, even Moses, in whom ye [all of you] trust."

The First Angel's Message – **Unwarranted Objections**

And then, Jesus emphasizes the writings of Moses;

"46 For had ye [all of you] believed Moses, ye would have believed Me: for he wrote of Me. 47 But if ye believe not his writings, how shall ye believe My words?" John 5:45-47

Did you hear that?
Christ the Creator of "all things" said that Moses wrote about Me and not about God the Father. Therefore we can agree with Christ the LORD of hosts when He says Moses wrote about Me; or we can call Christ a liar and disagree with Him and say like the objectors, "Moses wrote about God the Father."

It's your choice to make.

2)_____ Their second objection is found in the book of Genesis; it reads as follows:

"26 And God said, Let us make man in our image, after our likeness." Genesis 1:26

First, it should be noted that in verse twenty-six there was only a dialogue regarding the "image" of man; If man should be formed to look like the Creator and His Associate.

That's it!

Secondly, verse twenty-six does not deal with the creation of the heavens and of the earth as they are presented in Genesis chapter one. Therefore this verse cannot be applied to everything God the Christ had already created up until verses twenty-six. The only thing that was not created on the sixth day was man; otherwise everything else was created by Christ the Creator. Therefore up until that time period, there is no dialogue found anywhere in the Scriptures to reveal that there was a co-creator involved with Christ the Creator.

And thirdly, verse twenty-seven of Genesis chapter one deals with the creation of man; therefore the God who said "Let us make man in our Image" was none other than Christ the Creator because it was He who spoke the ecosystem of the earth, its inhabitants, as the previous creation verses have already stated. And then Christ created man as he is revealed to us in Genesis chapters one and two.

Nonetheless, if you were to consider verse twenty-six carefully, you will find, all Christ the Creator was asking His Associate, if it was all right to create man in "our image"? That's it! Asking to create man in "our image" does not involve the actual creation of man. And furthermore that statement does not involve a co-creator; verse twenty-seven explains why there was no co-creator involved in verse twenty-six or in verse twenty-seven.

The verse reads,

"27 So God created man in His image, in the image of God created He him; male and female created He them." Genesis 1:27

Did you notice? The verse says, "God created man in His image." And, the verse also says that God created man "in the image of God [Christ's Associate]." And to further clarify that it was God the Christ who created man, Moses uses the pronoun "He" to tell us that there was no co-creator involved in the creation of man. Moses says, "male and female created He them."

Did you hear that? Moses says, "God created He him; male and female created He them."

There is no confusion in the above verse regarding the creation of Adam and Eve. Christ the God of Abraham created "He them." As you can see, there is no statement in the above

The First Angel's Message – **Unwarranted Objections**

verse where it states we created. Read verse twenty-seven again and observe; there is no we or us anywhere to be found in the creation of man. But there are in confirmation, the pronouns "His" and "He" mentioned couple of times to specify that there was only one Creator involved in the creation of man.

To further confirm the fact that there was no co-creator involved with Christ the LORD of hosts, we are told,

"6 for in the image of God [Christ's Associate] made He man." Genesis 9:6

To clarify the verse, the verse will read as follows:

"6 for in the image of God [the Father] made He [Christ] man." Genesis 9:6

In addition we are also told that Christ the Creator created man by Himself by saying,

"6 And it repenteth the LORD that He had made man on the earth, and it grieved Him at His heart 7 And the LORD said, I will destroy man whom I have created from the face of the earth;" Genesis 6:6, 7

Did you notice? Christ the Creator said, "I will destroy man whom I have created." That's right, Christ the LORD of hosts said, "whom I have created." Therefore as per that statement and as per the previous verses, there was no co-creator involved with Christ the Creator in the creation of "all things."

As a result, Christ is the sole Creator of His universe; He did not need any help in the creation of the universe and man. If you think that Christ the Creator needed help by having someone to help Him, then you are putting limitation upon

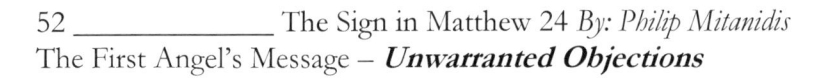

The First Angel's Message – **Unwarranted Objections**

Him.

Do you really want to do that!

If you do, then you are mocking the Creator because the prophet of Christ the Creator says, "Is there anything impossible for the LORD?"

3)_____ The other references that are given to support a co-creator are found in the New Testament verses where the objectors choose certain Bibles, which have the creation verses of the Greek text translated incorrectly.

Therefore, if you were to review some of these Bibles in the market place, you would notice that they not only contradict each other, but they also contradict the Greek inspired Scriptures.

Here are few examples:

"1 IN THE beginning [before all time] was the Word (d Christ), and the Word was with God, and the Word was God Himself. [Isa. 9:6]" "3 All things were made and came into existence through Him; and without Him was not even one thing made that has come into being." "10 He came into the world, and though the world was made through Him, the world did not recognize Him [did not know Him]." John 1:1, 3, 10 (Amp)

"1 In the beginning the Word already existed; the Word was with God, and the Word was God." "3 Through him God made all things; not one thing in all creation was made without him." "10 The Word was in the world, and though God made the world through him, yet the world did not recognize him." John 1:1, 3, 10 (TEV)

The First Angel's Message – **Unwarranted Objections**

"1 In the beginning was the one who is called the Word. The Word was with God and was truly God." "3 And with this Word, God created all things. Nothing was made without the Word." "10 The Word was in the world, but no one knew him, though God had made the world with his Word." John 1:1, 3, 10 (CEV)

If you look in verses three and ten, in the above three translations, you will observe that they all corroborate that somebody created "all things" and the "world" "through" the "Word" (Christ) as we know Him now in the New Testament by His character name.

But, if you read the Old King James Version of the Bible (OKJV), which is the closest translation of the Hebrew and Greek Scriptures that I know of, you will notice that it like the Greek Scriptures disagree with the above three Bible translations. (Amp.) (TEV) (CEV).

The Old King James Version reads as follows:

"1 IN the beginning was the Word, and the Word was with God, and the Word was God.

"3 All things were made by Him [Christ the Word of v.1]; and without Him [Christ] was not anything made that was made.

"10 He [Christ] was in the world, and the world was made by Him [Christ]." John 1:1, 3, 10 (OKJV)

Now take a good look in the above three verses of the (OKJV), and observe if the word "through" is present; obviously it is not. Verse three states that "All things were made by Him [Christ]." Likewise verse ten says the same thing.

The First Angel's Message – **Unwarranted Objections**

We are told that "He [Christ] was in the world, and the world was made by Him [Christ]." As you have observed, none of the verses say that somebody created "all things" and the "world" through Christ.

To further confirm the fact that the mistranslated word "through" does not exist in the Greek inspired Scriptures, look at verses three and ten in the following Greek text and observe the presence of the word δι' [by].

"3 Παντα δι' [by] αυτου εγειναν και χωρις αυτου δεν εγειναν ουδε εν το οποιον εγεινεν."

"10 Ητο εν τω κοσμω, και ο κοσμος εγεινε δι' [by] αυτου." Ιωαννην 1:3, 10 (Βιβλικη Εταιρεια) John 1:3, 10

As you can see the Greek word δι' [by] is present in the above two verses.

And to further confirm the fact that many of the Bible translators have altered the meaning of the New Testament creation verses by using the uninspired word "through," apostle Paul says in the Greek text "11 For of Him [Christ]…are all things" (Romans 11:36). Therefore, according to the Greek text ["εξ αυτου, και δι αυτου, και εις αυτου"], the creation of "all things" was "of Him [Christ]," "by [δι'] Him [Christ]," "for Him Christ]," and not of God the Father or of God the Holy Spirit or of anyone else. The fact that the creation of "all things" was "of Him [Christ]," Apostle Paul further added, "16 all things were created by [δι'] Him [Christ of v.15], and for Him [Christ]" (Colossians 1:16). Therefore the mistranslated word "through" should not be used as some Bible translators have taken the liberty to add in the New Testament creation verses.

A person should not delete the word of God or add his or

her own words. Therefore the Greek word δι' [by] should not be deleted from all of the creation verses that are found in the New Testament. There was a reason why God the Holy Spirit used the word δι' [by], and that reason, like the Old Testament prophets, the New Testament prophets believed that there is only one Creator; and as a result, they had to use the word δι' [by].

Therefore the translators should not have removed the word δι' [by], and used the uninspired word "through" in the creation verses.

I do not know if you know that there is a very strong condemnation in the Old and New Testaments to individuals who add, delete, or preach the Gospel of Jesus Christ willfully in error. The warning is as follows:

> "8 But though we, or an angel from heaven, preach any other gospel unto you than that which we have preached unto you, let him be accursed." Galatians 1:8

Did you hear that?

Very strong language, don't you think?

Nonetheless, by using the mistranslated word "through" in the creation verses of the New Testament it postures the New Testament against the Old Testament because nowhere in the Old Testament you will find in the creation verses where they state that somebody created "through" Christ the LORD of hosts or Christ the LORD of hosts created through somebody.

As a result, since there is no co-creator mentioned in any of the creation verses in the entire 66 books of the Bible, we can agree with the prophet Malachi and say,

> "10 Have we not all one father? Hath not one God created us? why do we deal treacherously every

The First Angel's Message – **Unwarranted Objections**

man against his brother by profaning the covenant of our fathers?" Malachi 2:10

So! Do you agree with Malachi the prophet of Christ the LORD of hosts that there is only "one God" who "created us"? Or do you disagree with him? But, if you agree with Malachi; then we can conclude that there is only one Creator, and that Creator, as per Scripture, is Christ the LORD of hosts who says,

"4 command them [the delegates, who came to Jerusalem] to say unto their masters, thus saith the LORD of hosts, the God of Israel; Thus shall ye [all of you] say unto your masters;

"5 I have made the earth, the man and the beast that are upon the ground, by My great power and by My outstretched arm," Jeremiah 27:4, 5

* * *   If you desire more detailed information on the subject of the Creator, creation, the pros and cons of the creation verses, translators, the Hebrew and Greek texts, and much, much more, please read my book "The Creator of Genesis 1:1 Who is He" by: *Philip Mitanidis*,   BEEHIVE PUBLISHING HOUSE INC. 2003"   * 1

~~~~~~~~~

Unfortunately, due to legal wrangling in the courtrooms, the majority of the translators who translate the Greek text to English, it appears that they are continuing to alter the word of the LORD of hosts to avoid

---

* 1   Mitanidis Philip *Moses Wrote About Me* BEEHIVE PUBLISHING HOUSE INC. 2013 edition , pp 247-257

The First Angel's Message – **Unwarranted Objections**

lawsuits. But, as much as they try to avoid and make void the Greek word δι' [by] in the Greek creation texts, they cannot eradicate the word of the LORD because the Greek text, just like the Hebrew text, will always remain to state the fact that Christ is the sole Creator of the universe and outside of the universe. Scripture says, "16 all things were created by [δι'] Him [Christ], and for Him [Christ]" (Colossians 1:16). So, be careful what translation you are using to base your faith in.

In conclusion, as per scripture, there is one Creator who created "all things" and is worshipped by the heavenly host (Nehemiah 9:6). Now because that message is not preached by the three humongous religious institutions, the first angel is admonishing us today to emulate the host of heaven; we are to:

"7 worship Him [Christ] that made heaven, and earth, and the sea, and the fountains of waters." Revelation 14:7

The "Great Tribulation"

Seeing that the "great tribulation" is going to divide the people of the entire world into two camps, one for Jesus Christ the LORD and the other for Satan, of what "great tribulation" is Jesus Christ the LORD of hosts talking about in Matthew 24:21; and what events would be taking place during the "great tribulation"?

The "great tribulation" Jesus is referring to is going to be brought about by the deceitful 2nd beast of Revelation 13:11 (More on this point later.); and by the support of the three humungous religious institutions (Muslims, Jews, and Christians), which claim that they believe in the Bible, but refuse to repent and adhere to the admonition that is given to them by Jesus Christ the LORD in Revelation 3:14-22. And because they refuse to repent and to preach the Gospel of Jesus Christ the LORD, Jesus is going to "spue" (Rev. 3:16) them out of His "mouth." And once Jesus "speu's" them out of His "mouth," they will turn with vengeance upon those individuals who will take Christ's council of Revelation 3:14-22, repent, accept the Gospel doctrine of Jesus Christ the LORD, and start propagating the Gospel of Jesus Christ throughout the world with the help of the three angels (Revelation 14:6-11) and with the help of God the Holy Spirit.

At first, persecution is going to be mild, as it is today; but once it becomes openly visible, by civil law, God's people and other nonconformists will experience the wrath of the second beast in the form of hate, beatings, starvation, prison camps, torture, loss of jobs, and animosity throughout the

The 3 Angel's Messages – **The Great Tribulation**

world.

It should be noted: Satan and his satanic agencies do not want the Gospel of Jesus Christ to be preached and bring hope to a perishing world. But, as you have read, Jesus said,

> "14 this gospel of the kingdom shall be preached in all the world for a witness unto all nations; and then shall the end come" (Matthew 24:14).

The reason why Satan and his satanic agencies do not want Christ's Gospel to be preached by willing hands is due to the fact that once the Gospel is preached to the entire world, "then shall the end come." And once the end comes, Satan, his evil angels, evil men, and evil women will be sealed to be cast into the lake of fire and burn into "ashes" (Matt. 25:41; Malachi 4:1-3). And that scenario is not welcomed by Satan, his evil angels, evil men, and evil women who delight in evil, practice evil, and worship Satan.

Moreover, persecution upon the repentant sinners will be unleashed upon them in order to discourage them from accepting the three angel's messages; and to prevent them from preaching the Gospel of Jesus Christ the LORD to a perishing human race. By persecuting the repentant sinners, Satan and his satanic agencies hope to stop the advancement of the Gospel, converts to Christ, or at least delay Christ's second coming.

Because of those few and other reasons, Satan and his satanic agencies, will eventually unleash the floodgates of evil persecution and death, by the hand of the civil laws, upon those who repent and accept the three angel's messages.

But, the Gospel of the three angel's messages cannot be stop. They have been commissioned with a sense of urgency. Jesus has spoken; He said,

"¹¹ I have spoken it, I will also bring it to pass; I have purposed it, I will also do it" (Isaiah 46:11).

And in regards to His Gospel, Jesus also said, "¹⁴ this gospel of the kingdom shall be preached in all the world for a witness unto all nations; and then shall the end come" (Matthew 24:14). And "this gospel of the kingdom" is preached today as you are reading this book; and it has made quite a few enemies; and at the same time, it also has brought quite a few repentant sinners to Christ. And because these repentant sinners have accepted Jesus Christ as their LORD God and Savior, they have picked up the banner of Christ the LORD and are preaching today the three angel's messages to a degenerating hopeless human beings who are headed to their eternal demise.

Therefore, as you have noticed in the news media, this "great tribulation" of Revelation 13:11-18, which has already started through out the world, by the 2nd beast (Britain & America) will continue to escalate into the "great tribulation." And once the death penalty of Revelation 13:15 is imposed upon God's people and upon the nonconformist by the religious and political enforcers of Satan the devil (the "dragon"), the persecution will accelerate upon the nonconformists.

So! Why is Revelation 13:11-18 the "great tribulation" of which Jesus is referring to and not another?

Here are few reasons why Revelation 13:11-18 is identified as the "great tribulation" of which Jesus is referring to.

1). Prophetically and literally, Revelation 13:11-18 is the only tribulation remaining that is not fulfilled before the "sign" of Christ takes place in heaven, and before the second coming of Christ takes place.

2). Prophetically and literally, Revelation 13:11-18 is the "great tribulation" because "immediately after the tribulation," the "sign" of Christ appears in the heaven for all to see (Matthew 24:29, 30); and that event has not occurred right after the previous tribulations that have taken place in the entire world's history and even right up until now.

3). Prophetically and literally, remember, "immediately after the great tribulation," the "sign" of Christ appears in heaven for all to see (Matthew 24:29, 30). And since the Gospel of Jesus Christ is preached, just before the "end comes" (Matthew 24:14), it means that the Gospel of Jesus and the "great tribulation" occur simultaneously and end simultaneously because the "sign" of Christ appears in heaven "immediately after the great tribulation" (Matthew 24:29, 30).

4). Another reason why Revelation 13:11-18 is the "great tribulation" is simply because it is said by Jesus that another tribulation after the "great tribulation" will not take place.
Here is His reference:

"21 For then shall be great tribulation, such as was not since the beginning of the world to this time, no, nor ever shall be." Matthew 24:21

Consequently because there will not be another tribulation after the "great tribulation" of Revelation 13:11- 18; we can conclude that the next major events are going to take place right after the "great tribulation" of Revelation 13:11-18.

The 3 Angel's Messages – **The Great Tribulation**

So! What are those major events that will take place right after the "great tribulation" ends?

Jesus gives the answer. He said, "29 Immediately after the tribulation, of those days shall the sun be darkened, and the moon shall not give her light, and the stars shall fall from heaven, and the powers of the heavens shall be shaken:"

And, after the heavens are shaken, Jesus says, "30 then shall appear the sign of the Son of man [Christ] in heaven." And when the wicked see the "sign" of Christ in heaven, we are told; "and then shall all the tribes of the earth mourn, and they shall see the Son of man coming in the clouds of heaven with power and great glory." Matthew 24:29, 30

After the "sign" of Christ appears in heaven for all the people of the earth to see, Christ's repentant people who have come through the "great tribulation" will be sealed and wait for Christ's second coming to take place.

> "1 And after these things I saw four angels standing on the four corners of the earth, holding the four winds of the earth, that the wind should not blow on the earth, nor on the sea, nor on any tree.
>
> "2 And I saw another angel ascending from the east, having the seal of the living God: and he cried with a loud voice to the four angels, to whom it was given to hurt the earth and the sea,
>
> "3 Saying, Hurt not the earth, neither the sea, nor the trees, till we have sealed the servants of our God in their foreheads." Revelation 7:1-3

Therefore, we can conclude that Revelation 13:11-18 is

The 3 Angel's Messages – **The Great Tribulation**

the "great tribulation" because the four points, mentioned above, go hand in hand; and prepare the way for Christ's 2nd coming with His holy angels to take place right after the plagues fall on the un-repented wicked and upon the ecosystem of the earth (Revelation 18:1-4).

So, how is the great tribulation (Revelation 13:11-18) described by Apostle John?

> He says; "11 And I beheld another beast coming up out of the earth; and he had two horns like a lamb, and he spake as a dragon. 12 And he exerciseth all the power of the first beast before him, and causeth the earth and them which dwell therein to worship the first beast, whose deadly wound was healed. 13 And he doeth great wonders, so that he maketh fire come down from heaven on the earth in the sight of men,
>
> "14 And deceiveth them that dwell on the earth by the means of those miracles which he had power to do in the sight of the beast; saying to them that dwell on the earth, that they should make an image to the beast, which had the wound by a sword, and did live.
>
> "15 And he had power to give life unto the image of the beast, that the image of the beast should both speak, and cause that as many as would not worship the image of the beast should be killed.
>
> "16 And he causeth all, both small and great, rich and poor, free and bond, to receive a mark in their right hand, or in their foreheads: 17 And that no man might buy or sell, save he that had the mark, or the name of the beast, or the number of his name. 18 Here is wisdom. Let him that hath understanding count the number of the beast: for it is the number of a man; and his number is Six hundred threescore and six."
> Revelation 13:11-18

The 3 Angel's Messages – **The Great Tribulation**

Now that you have a glimpse of the "great tribulation," it should be noted that you and I are living at the beginning of Revelation 13:12, and waiting for the 2nd beast (Britain & America) to mobilize the masses of the world "to worship the 1st beast [papacy], whose deadly wound was healed" (Revelation 13:12).

Although I have alluded as to the identity of the 1st beast and of the 2nd beast, let us look at the scripture references and see if the 1st beast is the papacy and the 2nd beast is (Britain & America)?

Looking at Revelation thirteen and verse eleven, Apostle John states that he saw "another beast." The reason he states that he saw "another beast," is due to the fact that he already saw and described the first beast in Revelation 13:1-3. And then he says that the second beast of v.11 "had two horns like a lamb." And the 2nd beast "spake as a dragon" (Revelation 13:11).

According to Scripture, the two horns represent "kingdoms" or "kings." (See Daniel 8:3-9, 15, 19-22.) And the "dragon" represents Satan the devil (Revelation 12:9).

Here is a quick summery of the identities of the beasts and of the horns that are mentioned by Daniel and Apostle John taken from my book called "Christians Headed into the Time of Trouble" *By Philip Mitanidis* BEEHIVE PUBLISHING HOUSE INC. 2007. pgs. 166-168

"Prophetically, "winds" represent strife, wars, and commotion, Jeremiah 25:32, 33. And, "water" represents populations or populated areas of people and tongues, Revelation 17:15.

When Daniel observed the four beasts coming out of the "sea" (Daniel 7:2-8), he observed each beast (kingdom) coming out from the previous kingdom. In other words, the four kingdoms came out of heavily

The 3 Angel's Messages – **The Great Tribulation**

populated kingdoms. Babylon came out of the heavily populated Middle East and Egypt. Medo-Persia came out of the Babylonian Empire. The Greek Empire came out of the Medo-Persian Empire; and the Roman Empire came out of the Greek Empire.

But, in Revelation thirteen, the second beast (v.11) with the two horns, did not come out from the "sea." He did not come out from the four empires or from any empires or conquered empires; the two-horned beast created his own kingdom.

So, what world empire or empires did not come out of an empire or out of any conquered empires, after the first beast's head (pope) was wounded in 1798 AD by the French army? (See Revelation 13:3.)

Historically, it was the empire of North America, which arose in the late seventeenth century.

If you recall, England dominated North America until the late seventeen hundred when its citizens split North America into two nations.

The struggle for independence began in 1775; and in 1777, thirteen States assembled in Congress and adopted the Articles of Confederation. And when the war between Britain and the colonies ended in 1783, the Constitution was framed in 1787; and ratified in July 26, 1788 by eleven States.

The British retained the northern part of the country, now called Canada; and the United States (US) retained the southern part of the country now called America, but better known as the United States of America (USA).

Although Britain and the United States are identified as separate countries, you would be surprised to know that England and the USA have been working together ever since the eighteen forties—in England's favor. You will find that they both build their war arsenals together. They have joint war exercises. They share their technology. They even have their armed forces personnel manning and overseeing each other's command posts. In fact, the Canadian armed forces and the American armed forces frequently have joint and separate war exercises on each other's land. And as the war games go on in each other's land, a person can readily see the foreign flag flying above the sovereign's flag.

For example; during the 911 attack (September 11, 2001) on the twin towers, in New York, the individual who manned the command post in NORAD (North American Aerospace Defense Control) was Lt. Rick Findley, a Canadian officer whose allegiance is to the Queen of England. He was the one who gave the command to the United States armed forces, which implemented the American and the British forces into combat ready; not only on US soil, but also throughout the world; and that included air, submarines, and ships. These forces, under the command of a British officer, were ready to strike the enemy in retaliation.

They listened and looked, and looked in their radars, satellites, graphs, infrared, telescopes, and in all manner of electronic gadgetry; but they could not see their enemy! That is why during 911 nothing moved for a long period of time on land and sea. They were motionless; watching for their enemy's movements. But with all of their sophisticated power, Britain and America were not able to find their enemy.

Can you imagine; while the Americans and the British armed forces were in such a state of high alert, it was a foreign British officer who implemented and oversaw the activities of the American armed forces,

The 3 Angel's Messages – ***The Great Tribulation***

during the most crucial time of her war!

And ever since that time (911), a person can readily see in the news media that it is no secret of how the British and the Americans have fought and are fighting together the American war against the insurgency of Islam.

Today, there is no power on earth such as Britain and America that can fit the prophecy so apply— religiously and politically.

Therefore, according to Revelation 13:11 these two kingdoms, the British and the Americans, who came unto the world scene in the late seventeen hundred, in North America, are the two horns of the second beast of Revelation 13:11." ** 2

Now that we know who is the 2nd beast, we can ask who or what is the first beast of Revelation 13:1-3?

To answer, if you were to look at the rise and fall of all of the kingdoms and nations after the fall of the Roman Empire in 476 AD, you will notice, in particular in Europe, there rose ten kingdoms out of the rubble of the Roman Empire. And no sooner those ten kingdoms rose and flourished, a political and religious power came on the scene, and by the use of the hand of the civil and political powers subdued three kingdoms and began to rule Europe in 538 AD by the intimidation of the religious and civil legislature. And that power, historically and Scripturally, is identified as the Roman Catholic Church, but more specifically, the popes of the church.

And once the popes began to flex their political and religious muscles upon the people, in those days, many people

---

** 2   Mitanidis Philip *Christians Headed Into the Time of Trouble* BEEHIVE PUBLISHING HOUSE INC. 2007 pp 166-168

did not want to conform to the dictates of the popes because they did not like the pope's religious policies or the political policies that were handed down upon them. Therefore many rebelled. And in order to eliminate the uncompromising insurgence, the popes began to persecute, torture, burn to the stake, bury alive, beat, jail, starve, and kill the nonconformists right up until the time Napoleon Bonaparte captured the pope in 1798 AD and took him to France and imprisoned him. The pope died there two years later.

But that did not stop the Roman Catholic Church from choosing another pope. And strangely enough, another pope was chosen, while the Protestant Reformers who were persecuted, stood by and allowed the Roman Catholic Church to continue to enthrone popes, and without remorse persecute the Jews and others in Spain right up until 1860 AD. And even worse, today, to Christ's anathema and abomination, the popes who rise from the Vatican are considered by many Protestants as spiritual leaders of the world, even though their church doctrine in inundated with paganism and false representation of Christ and of the Gospel of Jesus Christ the LORD.

<u>Scripturally,</u> the popes and the Roman Catholic Church (1st beast) were prophetically forecasted about 900 years before they came on the world scene. Nonetheless, to begin with, the papacy and their evil works are identified as follows: We are told, "17 These great beasts [of Daniel 7:3-8], which are four, are four kings, which shall arise out of the earth" (Daniel 7:17). They are identified as the Babylonian Empire, the Medo-Persian Empire, the Greek Empire, and the Roman Empire.

And in reference to the fourth beast (Roman Empire), Daniel the prophet of the LORD says,

> "19 Then I would know the truth of the fourth beast, which was diverse from all the others, exceeding dreadful, whose teeth were of iron,

and his nails of brass; which devoured, brake in pieces, and stamped the residue with his feet;

"20 And of the ten horns that were in his head, and of the other which came up, and before whom three fell; even of that horn that had eyes, and a mouth that spake very great things, whose look was more stout than his fellows.

> "₂₁ I beheld, and the same horn made war with the saints, and prevailed against them" Daniel 7:19-21

After seeing the vision (Daniel 7:3-14), Daniel wanted to know to who or what the fourth beast, the ten horns, and the little horn that came up out of the ten horns, and the three kings or kingdoms it overthrew are referring to? Therefore Daniel asked one of the angels who stood near by (vs. 15, 16) to reveal and explain the meaning of all that was shown to him.

> "₂₃ Thus he [the angel] said [to Daniel], The fourth beast shall be the fourth kingdom upon earth, which shall be diverse from all kingdoms, and shall devour the whole earth, and shall tread it down, and break it in pieces."

The "fourth kingdom upon earth," after the Greek Empire 331 BC - 168 BC, was the Roman Empire 168 BC -476 AD.

> "₂₄ And the ten horns out of this kingdom are ten kings that shall arise and another shall rise after them; and he shall be diverse from the first, and he shall subdue three kings." Daniel 7:23, 24

After the Roman Empire fell in 476 AD, ten kings or kingdoms rose up in Europe from its rubble. But another king or kingdom that was diverse or different from the others was to rise and "subdue three kings" out of the ten "kings" or kingdoms if you like. The three kings that were subdued by the diverse king were the "East Goths," which were located north of Italy. The "West Goths," which were located west of Italy.

The 3 Angel's Messages – **The Great Tribulation**

And the "Vandals," which were located south of Italy at the northern tip of Africa. These three kings or kingdoms were dethroned by the armies of Emperor Justinian who was asked by the pope of the Roman Catholic Church to go and do his bidding. Thus the pope by the political and civil arm ousted the three kings, and in essence, took control of Europe.

Consequently because the pope acquired the political arm to do its evil biding; and is religiously inclined, he is identified as the "diverse" king from the other 10 "kings."

But, the pope's power did not stop the use of the political and civil arm upon the kings he did not like; he also began to use those powers to persecute, torture, starve, bunt to the stake, imprison, and kill all of those individuals who did not conform to his religious and political dictates.

And, if that was not evil enough, we are told,

> "25 And he [the pope] shall speak great words against the most High [Christ], and shall wear out the saints of the most High [Christ], and think to change times and laws: and they shall be given into his hand until a time and times and the dividing of time." Daniel 7:25

As you have read above, the pope is going to "speak great words against the most High [Christ]."

Did you notice the little word "against"?

That is right; speaking "great words against" Christ the LORD of hosts is an outright blasphemy. Saying anything "against" Christ or contrary to Christ's words is blasphemy because Christ is represented as a liar. Therefore, as an example, the following papal doctrinal beliefs are blasphemous. They are "great words against" Christ because the popes claim that the priesthood is still in force. That Easter eggs, bunnies, ash Wednesday, Christmas, icons, candles, rosaries, paying your

The 3 Angel's Messages – ***The Great Tribulation***

way to heaven, purgatory, the dead are not dead, hell, worshipping idols and dead saints, choosing to venerate Mary, Mary sitting in heaven and asking favors from Christ, and the like are all blasphemous "great words against the most High [Christ]."

And, if that is not blasphemous enough, speaking "great words against the Most High [Christ], Adam Clarke adds:

> "'He shall speak as if he were 'God.' So St. Jerome quotes from Symmachus. To none can this apply so well or so fully as to the popes of Rome. They have assumed infallibility, which belongs only to God. They profess to forgive sins, which belongs only to God. They profess to open and shut heaven, which belongs only to God. They profess to be higher than all the kings of the earth, which belongs only to God. And they go *beyond* God in pretending to loose whole nations from their oath of allegiance to their kings, which such kings do not please them. And they go *against* God when they give indulgences or sin. This is the worst of all blasphemies." *** 3

As per Christ Gospel, mortal sinful drenched man cannot forgive his own sins or forgive another person's sins. And the reason why we cannot forgive someone else's sins is due to the fact that when we sin, we sin against Christ the LORD of hosts. That is why only Christ the LORD can

---

*** 3   Adam Clarke, *Commentary on the Old Testament*, vol. iv, p.596, note on Daniel 7:25

forgive your sins and my sins. Sin is a personal act between the sinner and Christ the LORD. Therefore the popes of Vatican city cannot forgive anyone's sins; and for the popes to claim that they can and do is an outright blasphemous lie, as the historians above indicated.

In addition, we are told that the pope (horn of v.20 & 25) shall "think to change times and laws" (v.25).

So! What "times and laws" did the pope "think" to have changed?

According to Christ's Gospel, the times and laws the popes "think" that they have changed are as follows: They "think" that they have changed the "time" duration of the Levitecall priesthood. By implementing the priesthood, they "think" that they have changed the "time" duration of the ceremonial law. By implementing the priesthood and the ceremonial law it means that the sacrificial lambs should continue; and it also means that a person has to choose between the sacrificial lamb and Christ death on Calvary's cross for one's salvation. And, it should be noted; the priests of the Roman Catholic church are not from the tribe of Levi, and neither is the pope who acts as the high priest. By changing the fourth commandment from Saturday to Sunday, the popes "think" that they have changed the "law" (Decalogue, Exodus 20:2-17), the "time" duration, and the holy day. By changing the fourth commandment from Saturday to Sunday, the popes "think" that they have changed the "law," and the "time" duration of the day. You see Saturday, according to the fourth commandment (Exodus 20:8-11) is kept holy from Friday's sunset to Saturday's sunset. * (Continued on page 76).

The 3 Angel's Messages – **The Great Tribulation**

CHRIST'S TEN COMMANDMENTS READ AS FOLLOWS:

i

"3 Thou [you] shalt have no other gods before Me.

ii

"4 Thou [you] shalt not make unto thee any graven image, or any likeness of any thing that is in heaven above, or that is in the earth beneath, or that is in the water under the earth: 5 Thou [you] shalt not bow down thyself [yourself] to them, nor serve them: for I the LORD thy [your] God am a jealous God, visiting the iniquity of the fathers upon the children unto the third and fourth generation of them that hate Me; 6 And shewing mercy unto thousands of them that love Me, and keep My commandments.

iii

"7 Thou [you] shalt not take the name of the LORD thy God in vain; for the LORD will not hold him guiltless that taketh His name in vain.

iv

"8 Remember the sabbath day, to keep it holy. 9 Six days shalt thou labour, and do all thy work: 10 But the seventh day is the sabbath of the LORD thy God: in it thou shalt not do any work, thou, nor thy son, nor thy daughter, thy manservant, nor thy maidservant, nor thy cattle, nor thy stranger that is within thy gates: 11 For in six days the LORD made heaven and earth, the sea, and all that in them is, and rested the seventh day: wherefore the LORD blessed the sabbath day, and hallowed it.

v

"12 Honour thy father and thy mother: that thy days may be long upon the land which the LORD thy God giveth thee.

vi

"13 Thou [you] shalt not kill.

vii

"14 Thou [you] shalt not commit adultery.

viii

"15 Thou [you] shalt not steal.

ix

"16 Thou [you] shalt not bear false witness against thy neighbour.

x

"17 Thou [you] shalt not covet thy neighbour's house, thou shalt not covet thy neighbour's wife, nor his manservant, nor his maidservant, nor his ox, nor his ass, nor any thing that is thy neighbour's" (Exodus 20:3-17).

THE POPE'S TEN COMMANDMENTS READ AS FOLLOWS:

i
I am the Lord thy God. Thou [you] shalt not have Strange gods before me.

ii
Thou shalt not take the name of the Lord thy God in vain.

iii
Remember thou keep holy the Sabbath day.

iv
Honor thy father and thy mother.

v
Thou shalt not kill.

vi
Thou shalt not commit adultery.

vii
Thou shalt not steal.

viii
Thou shalt not bear false witness against thy Neighbor.

ix
Thou shalt not covet thy neighbor's wife.

x
Thou shalt not covet thy neighbor's goods.

The 3 Angel's Messages – **The Great Tribulation**

*(From page 73) But, the pope's Sunday is kept holy, by some, from Friday 12:00 AM to Sunday's sunset? And others keep Sunday holy from Friday 12:00 AM to Sunday 12:00 AM. By removing the second commandment (idol worship) completely from the Decalogue (Exodus 20:2-17), the popes "think" that they have changed the "law," and the "time" duration. By splitting the tenth commandment into two, to make up for the loss of the 2nd commandment, the popes "think" that they have changed the "time" duration and the 10 Commandments. And by implementing pagan rights and worship, the popes "think" that they have changed the "times" and the "law" (Decalogue), and so on.

Although the popes of Vatican city "think" they can change the "times" and the "laws" of Christ the LORD of hosts, it cannot be done.

Do you honestly think that helpless wretched evil stricken mortal man, who claims infallibility and erodes into dust, and at the end dies like the rest of the human race, can change anything that goes out of the mouth of Christ the LORD of hosts?

If you think so; all I can say, you like the popes are deceived and living in la, la land somewhere.

Man can "think" all he wants that he can change Christ's Gospel and the 10 Commandments. But, in fact they will remain intact eternally because in Christ's kingdom sin does not exist (1 John 3:4).

Moreover, we are also told that the pope(s) of the Roman Catholic Church,

> "25 shall wear out the saints of the Most High [Christ]" (Daniel 7:25).

After battling the two Arian kings for nearly twenty years in Europe, and defeating them for the pope, Emperor

The Sign in Matthew 24 *By: Philip Mitanidis* _____ 77
The 3 Angel's Messages – **The Great Tribulation**

Justinian gave the throne of Caesar and Caesar's palaces to the pope in 538 AD; and made the pope the "head of all churches" and the "corrector of heresy's."

By empowering the pope and the popes that followed in the Roman Catholic Church, they were emboldened to use the political and civil powers to their advantage.

And when insurgence, protestors, and nonconformists to the Vatican law began to multiply through out the land, the popes began to flex their muscles through the political and civil arm, in order to quell the uprisings, and the protestors who protested to the pope's pagan theology and for taking away their freedom to worship as they chose. And when other people learned through the protestors about the Bible doctrine, they too lost reverence for the fraudulent popes who claim infallibility and began to leave the Roman Catholic Church by the thousands.

Seeing that the church was hemorrhaging members very rapidly and going to their newly found faith, the popes decreed that all those who speak against the Roman Catholic church and its doctrinal beliefs and teach otherwise, they shall be prosecuted. And, if they would not conform to the dictates of the papacy and to the papal doctrine, they would be killed in the name of "heresy."

Perhaps the above words might not have much impact upon you; but, if your family's tree is derived from the Protestant Reformers, you might be familiar with the persecution, which caused millions to be tortured, beaten, hanged, starved, burnt to the stake, beheaded, killed, buried alive, and so on. And how the nonconformists lost their possessions to the papacy—land, property, money, loved ones, and so on. Millions perished by the pope's use of the political and civil arm. The popes left a long and wide trail by the blood of the nonconformists, and by the blood of God's people throughout the papal history, all in the name of "heresy."

The 3 Angel's Messages – **The Great Tribulation**

But, if you are not familiar with the papacy's callous inhumane vindictive evil treatment upon those who found out that the Roman Catholic church's Christian doctrine is intertwine with paganism and the false teaching, here is a brief glimpse of what was going on between the popes and the protestors, during the Reformation, between 538 AD to 1798 AD, all in the name of "heresy."

> Albert Barnes says,: "Can anyone doubt that this is true of the papacy? The Inquisition, the 'persecutions of the Waldenses;' The ravages of the Duke of Alva; the fires of Smithfield; the tortures of Goa—indeed, the whole history of the papacy may be appealed to in proof that this is applicable to that power. If anything *could* have 'worn out the saints of the Most High'— could have cut them off from the earth so that evangelical religion would have become extinct, it would have been the persecutions of the papal power. In the year 1208, a crusade was proclaimed by Pope Innocent III against the Waldenses and Albigenses, in which a million of men perished. From the beginning of the order of the Jesuits, in the year 1540, to 1580, nine hundred thousand were destroyed. One hundred and fifty thousand perished by the Inquisition in thirty years. In the Low Countries fifty thousand persons were hanged, beheaded, burned, and buried alive, for the crime of heresy, within the space of thirty-eight years from the edict of Charles V against the Protestants, to the peace of Chateau Cambreses in 1559. Eighteen thousand suffered by the hand of the executioner in the space of five

The 3 Angel's Messages – **The Great Tribulation**

years and a half during the administration of the Duke of Alva. Indeed, the slightest acquaintance with the history of the papacy will convince any one that what is here said of 'making war with the saints' (verse 21), and 'wearing out the saints of the Most High' (verse 25), is strictly applicable to that power, and will accurately describe its history." **** 4

Now that you got a glimpse of the evil atrocities the papacy has committed through out their history, now we can ask, how long did the deadly persecution continue to be imposed upon all of the nonconformists and upon God's people who refused to conform to the dictates of the popes?

According to verse twenty-five of Daniel chapter seven, persecution by the papacy was to continue for 1,260 years.

Here is the reference and the calculation: "and they shall be given into his hand until a time and times and the dividing of time." Daniel 7:25

The time period ("a time and times and the dividing of time"), as per the above verse, is calculated as follows: In scripture, a month has thirty days. And a year has twelve months. Therefore a year has $30 \times 12 = 360$ days. And a day in prophetic calculations equals to one year (Ezekiel 4:6). As a result, as per the above verse "a time" (30×12) equals to 360 years. And "times" (2×360) equals to 720 years. And "the dividing of time" ($360/2$) equals to 180 years. And the total of the above times ($360 + 720 + 180$) equals to 1,260 years.

Consequently, as per verse 25 and verse 21 of Daniel 7, the popes were to "wear out the saints of the Most High

---

**** 4 Albert Barnes, *Notes on Daniel*, p. 328, comment on Daniel 7:25

The 3 Angel's Messages – **The Great Tribulation**

[Christ]," and make "war with the saints, and prevailed against them" for 1,260 years. Historically and scripturally, they did, starting from 538 AD to 1798 AD and beyond in some countries on the globe.

And, in reference to the 1st beast of Revelation 13:1-3, Apostle John also gives the same time duration of the papacy's persecution upon the nonconformist as Daniel does. He says, "5 And there was given unto him a mouth speaking great things and blasphemies; and power was given unto him to continue forty and two months" (Revelation 13:5).

The calculation as per verse five above is as follows: "forty and two months" equals 42 months. And since there are 30 days in a Biblical month, we multiply 30 days per month by 42 months and that gives us 1,260 days. And since a day in a prophetic time equals to a year (Ezekiel 4:6), the calculations brings us to 1,260 years.

As you can see, Apostle John's calculation is the same as Daniel's 1,260 years calculation. We are told that the 1st beast persecuted and killed the saints of Jesus Christ the LORD for 1,260 years.

Apostle John writes:

> "6 And he opened his mouth in blasphemy against God, to blaspheme his name, and his tabernacle, and them that dwell in heaven. 7 And it was given unto him to make war with the saints, and to overcome them: and power was given him over all kindreds, and tongues, and nations. 8 And all that dwell upon the earth shall worship him, whose names are not written in the book of life of the Lamb [Christ] slain from the foundation of the world." Revelation 13:6, 7

The 3 Angel's Messages – **The Great Tribulation**

Although the persecution and death to a large degree had stopped during the 1900 AD, Christ's testimony reveals that the papacy's evil persecution and killing would resurface again. And that is why Apostle John was given the prophetic events in the book of Revelation. He was to warn the human race that the pope(s) would strike again with his wicked political and religious agenda to eradicate all those who would not conform to his wishes.

In reference to the first beast, the prophet of the LORD warns; "his deadly wound was healed" (Rev. 13:3).

So! The above begs the question; after the death of the imprisoned pope in 1798, the "wound was healed" (a new pope installed), where do we find the prophecy, which reveals that the pope's evil agenda would be imposed again upon all of the people on planet earth, only this time with all out evil vengeance?

Consider the following, the little horn (papacy) of verses 8, 20, 23-25, of Daniel chapter seven who dethroned three kingdoms, is continuously represented in Revelation 13 as the enemy of the saints. And he is identified as the first beast of Revelation 13:1-10. And the reason he is identified as the 1st beast is due to the fact that when you mirror the beasts of Daniel chapter seven to Revelation 13:1-10, you would find that Apostle John picks up where Daniel left off with his presentation in Daniel chapter seven.

So! Let us mirror Daniel's presentation with that of John's presentation and see if they are the same?

Here are the identities of the beasts found in Daniel 7:3-8:

The 1st beast was "like a lion," and "had eagle's wings" (v.4).

The 2nd beast was "like to a bear, and it raised up itself on one side, and it had three ribs in the mouth of it between the teeth of it" (v.5).

The 3 Angel's Messages – ***The Great Tribulation***

> The 3rd beast was "like a leopard, which had upon the back of it four wings of a fowl; the beast had also four heads" (v.6).
> The 4th beast was "dreadful and terrible, and strong exceedingly; and it had great iron teeth: it devoured and brake in pieces, and stamped the residue with the feet of it: and it was diverse from all the beasts that were before it; and it had ten horns" (v.7).
> And, from the 4th beast's head, came out ten horns.
> And from the ten horns, "behold, there came up among them another little horn, before whom there were three of the first horns plucked up by the roots: and, behold, in this horn were eyes like the eyes of man, and a mouth speaking great things" (Daniel 7: 8).

Now that you have considered what the four beasts of Daniel 7 look like, in the above verses; and what came out of the fourth beast's head, at this point compare these beasts with the first beast of Revelation 13:1-3 and see if they match?

Here are the references,

> Apostle John says, "1 And I stood upon the sand of the sea, and saw a beast rise up out of the sea, having seven heads and ten horns, and upon his horns ten crowns, and upon his heads the name of blasphemy.

> "2 And the beast which I saw was like unto a leopard, and his feet were as the feet of a bear, and his mouth as the mouth of a lion: and the dragon gave him his power, and his seat, and great authority.

The 3 Angel's Messages – **The Great Tribulation**

"3 And I saw one of his heads as it were wounded to death; and his deadly wound was healed: and all the world wondered after the beast" (Revelation 13:1-3).

Daniel in his presentation of Daniel 7 concluded with the fourth best's ten horns and the single stout horn that had eyes and a mouth, which "spake very great thing" (Daniel 7:20, 23-25). And, Apostle John picked up where Daniel left off by saying, "1 And I stood upon the sand of the sea, and saw a beast rise up out of the sea, having seven heads and ten horns, and upon his horns ten crowns, and upon his heads the name of blasphemy" (Revelation 13:1).

Now notice what Daniel says in the following verses about the horns, and compare them with what Apostle John

The 3 Angel's Messages – ***The Great Tribulation***

says in the above verse (v.1).

> "₂₀ And of the ten horns that were in his head, and of the other which came up, and before whom three fell; even of that horn that had eyes, and a mouth that spake very great things, whose look was more stout than his fellows."

And then the angel explains,

> "₂₄ And the ten horns out of this kingdom [4th ^{k} kingdom] are ten kings that shall arise: and another shall rise after them; and he shall be diverse from the first, and he shall subdue three kings" (Daniel 7:20, 24).

Thus, the angel's explanation to Daniel in the above verses and in comparison to Revelation 13:1, 2, are as follows: The "ten horns" of Daniel 7:20 "that were in his head" are the "ten kings" in Daniel 7:24. Likewise, these "ten horns" that are in the beast's seven heads of Revelation 13:1 are identified by Apostle John as "kings" by the use of "ten crowns" that are on the beast's ten "horns." There are seven "crowns" on the 7 horns of the "seven heads" of the beast; and three "crowns" on the three horns that are on the main head of the beast. The three horns on the main head of the beast of Revelation 13:1 with "crowns" upon them are the three "kings" the 1st beast overturned. And the other seven heads with each a horn on their heads, and with a crown on top of each horn, are seven "kings." Daniel says the same thing; out of the ten horns "three fell," Daniel 7:20 and he, the little horn, "shall subdue three kings" Daniel 7:20. In addition, Apostle John adds; and "upon his heads the name of blasphemy."

"₆ And he opened his mouth in blasphemy against

The 3 Angel's Messages – **The Great Tribulation**

God, to blaspheme His name, and His tabernacle, and them that dwell in heaven" (Revelation 13:1, 6).

Likewise Daniel says the same thing; the little horn had "a mouth that spake very great things" Daniel 7:20, and "25 he shall speak great words against the most High" Daniel 7:25.

After describing the horns of the first beast, Apostle John collates the description of the four beats of Daniel 7:3-8, and lumps them all into one body, and says, "2 And the beast which I saw was like unto a leopard, and his feet were as the feet of a bear, and his mouth as the mouth of a lion" (Revelation 13:2).

Apostle John's description of the beast, which he saw coming out of the water, as you have read above, is a collection of what Daniel describes in chapter seven. He says, the 1st beast was "like a lion," and "had eagle's wings" (v.4). The 2nd beast was "like to a bear, and it raised up itself on one side, and it had three ribs in the mouth of it between the teeth of it" (v.5). The 3rd beast was "like a leopard."

The 4th beast was "dreadful and terrible, and strong exceedingly; and it had great iron teeth: it devoured and brake in pieces, and stamped the residue with the feet of it: and it was diverse from all the beasts that were before it; and it had ten horns" (v.7).

Since the description of the first beast of Revelation 13:1-3, by Apostle John, is identical to Daniel's description of the beasts and horns in Daniel 7:3-8, 15-25, we can conclude that the first beast of Revelation 13:1-10 is a continuation of Daniel's vision, which he saw in chapter seven.

Therefore we can conclude that the first beast of Revelation 13:1-10 refers to none other than the kingdom of the papacy that is identified as the "little horn," which overthrew "three kings" and executed the nonconformists by the millions with the civil executioner's had from 538 AD to 1798 AD. The little horn (papacy) persecuted, tortured, beheaded, killed, and usurped land, money, houses, businesses, children, animals, etc., etc., for 1,260 years, in the name of "heresy," all because people would not bow down their knee to the dictates of the pope's pagan religious and political doctrine.

And this same power, the first beast of Revelation 13:1-10, is going to resurface during the "great tribulation" as an international political and religious power that would resume its evil inhumane persecution upon those who would not conform to his political and religious doctrines. And even worse, it is going to blaspheme God and God's name and those who live in heaven.

Can you comprehend his deliberate evil attitude?
Here is the reference. Apostle John writes,

"4 And the woman [city, Rev. 17:18] was arrayed in purple and scarlet colour, and decked with gold and precious stones and pearls, having a golden cup in her hand full of abominations and filthiness of her fornication: 5 And upon her forehead was a name written, MYSTERY, BABYLON THE GREAT, THE MOTHER OF HARLOTS AND ABOMINATIONS OF THE EARTH. 6 And I saw the woman drunken with the blood of the saints, and with the blood of the martyrs of Jesus" (Revelation 17:4-6).

Did you notice? Apostle John says, "6 And I saw the woman [Rev. 17:18] drunken with the blood of the saints, and with the blood of the martyrs of Jesus" (Rev. 17:6).

So! Who is going to give "power" to the 1st beast

The 3 Angel's Messages – **The Great Tribulation**

(pope) over "all kindreds, and tongues, and nations" to persecute the "martyrs of Jesus," and when?

According to Revelation 13:12, 15, the 2nd beast (Britain & America) is going to give the 1st beast (pope) "power" over "all kindreds, and tongues, and nations" during the "great tribulation."

Like before, persecution will begin with vengeance upon the nonconformists, as it did during the persecution, from 538 AD to 1798 AD, upon the protesters and during the Protestant Reformation. Although at that time, the protestors fled Europe from the persecutory power of the papacy, now during the "great tribulation" because the "great tribulation" is going to be a worldwide event, the persecuted will have nowhere to flee. During the last tribulation (Revelation 13:1-8, Napoleon Bonaparte, the French general intervened, captured the pope in 1798 AD, and took the pope to France and put him in jail where he died in 1800 AD (Revelation 13:3) that the persecution stopped to a large degree.

But, the papacy at that time did not give up upon their agenda to control the masses of the world by their political and religious means. That goal is still at the front burner. That is why the papacy pursued after the protestors wherever the protestors fled to, by sending their priests and nuns and members of their church to infiltrate the Protestant's political and civil offices, in order to set political laws to the pope's favor. The priests and nuns were also to spy on all that they could, and to collect information against outsiders, and even on their own congregations. One method of spying that is used effectively, is to bring people into the confession box and tell the priest of the various acts he or she did or heard.

Today, the pope's men and women have infiltrated the political and religious arena and are setting up laws in the pope's favor. And in the midst's of all this, the Protestants are not objecting to their evil deceptive works. And because the

The 3 Angel's Messages – **The Great Tribulation**

Protestants are not objecting to what the Roman Catholic church is doing, the Protestant Church is suffering and consuming in its own consequences politically and religiously. In fact Evangelism has eroded so badly throughout the Christian world that now Christians are not allowed to pray publicly in the name of Jesus Christ the LORD of hosts. They are told to pray in the name of God, what ever that means?

But, if the word "God" refers to God the Father, don't these church leaders and policy makers know that no man can pray directly to God the Father? If they do, their prayers are not going to be heard. Don't they know that? Don't they know that Jesus Christ the LORD cannot be bypassed or excluded from our prayers? Jesus said,

> "6 no man cometh unto the Father but by Me" (John 14:6).

What part of Christ's statement do they not understand to say to people that they cannot pray to God the Father in the name of Jesus Christ the LORD of hosts?

If they know, why are they lying to the public?

Are these policy makers above Christ the LORD?

And, if that is not bad enough, today many Evangelical Christian churches support the direct prayer to God the Father. And even worse, we hear that many of these churches already made a commitment to go back to the papacy.

Do they really want to forfeit their salvation that is only given by Jesus Christ the LORD and choose to openly live in sin with the 1st beast and with the 2nd beast and become the persecutors and killers of all who are holy?

Do they really want to be like the 1st beast and the 2nd beast?

Why?

What are they thinking?

The Sign in Matthew 24 *By: Philip Mitanidis*
The 3 Angel's Messages – ***The Great Tribulation***

Nonetheless, now that we know who is the first beast of Revelation 13:1-10, and who is the second beast of Revelation 13:11, and that the "dragon" (Satan, Rev. 12:9) gives the "seat, "power," and "authority," to the first beast of Revelation 13:2 and power to the 2nd beast of Revelation 13:11, now, we can consider the literal sequential events of the "great tribulation" (Revelation 13:11-18) of which Jesus is talking about in Matthew 24:21, and how the 1st beast is going to rise in power again, and how these vindictive events affect you and me.

Here are <u>the literal sequential events of the "great tribulation,"</u> starting from Revelation 13:11, which will effect you in one way or another.

The 2nd beast _____ *"he spake as a dragon."*

Apostle John writes,

"11 And I beheld another beast coming up out of the earth; and he had two horns like a lamb, and he spake as a dragon." Revelation 13:11

In the above verse Apostle John "beheld another beast." He makes that statement because he already saw a beast previously in Revelation 13:1-3. Therefore, the first beast, which Apostle John saw in Revelation 13:1-3, as we studied, is the papacy. And the second beast with the two horns, which John saw (v.11) is Britain and America. And the "dragon," which Apostle John saw, is Satan the devil.
Here is the reference:

"9 And the great dragon was cast out, that old serpent, called the Devil, and Satan, which deceiveth the whole world: he was cast out into the earth, and his angels were cast out with him" (Revelation 12:9).

In reference to the 2nd beast (Britain and America) of Revelation 13:11, as you have read, Apostle John warns and says, "he spake as a dragon."

So! How is the 2nd beast going to speak like the "dragon" (Satan)?

If you recall, during the last tribulation (Rev. 13:5-8), which lasted for 1,260 years (Rev. 13:5), the dragon (Satan) was speaking through the first beast (the papacy) because,

"2 the dragon gave him his power, and his seat, and great authority" (Revelation 13:2).

Therefore the 2nd beast (Britain and America) will also speak as the first beast was speaking because the prophet of the LORD says, "he [the 2nd beast] speaks as a dragon." And speaking as a "dragon" is to speak with lies, deceit, dishonesty, fabrication, malice, wickedness, and with self-serving authority at the cost of the rest of the world, in order to amass allies to his cause and use them to his benefit. And surprisingly, the second beast (Britain and America), today, already has 195 countries supporting his evil self-serving oppressive cause, which is, like the 1st beast (papacy), to rule the world through his supporters.

The 2nd beast __ 1). *"he exerciseth all the power of the first beast before him."* 2). *And causes "the earth and them which dwell therein to worship the first beast."*

And while the 2nd beast (Britain & America) speaks, like the dragon (Satan), with lies and deceit, he will

The 3 Angel's Messages – **The Great Tribulation**

> "₁₂ exerciseth all the power of the first beast before him, and causeth the earth and them which dwell therein to worship the first beast, whose deadly wound was healed [Rev. 13:3]" (Revelation 13:12).

In the above verse (v.12), we are warned that the 2nd beast (Britain & America) will exercise all the power and authority of the 1st beast (papacy); which is, the use of the local and international armed forces, the local and international police, the local and international civil laws, which he has a hand in forming, and the local and international judges to prosecute and persecute, beat, jail, torture, defame, and confiscate the people's possessions, if the people of planet earth would not do as he says or when he insists that all of the people of the world worship the first beast.

The 2nd beast ___ *"he maketh fire come down from heaven on the earth in the sight of men"*

And while the 2nd beast, like the 1st beast, continues to get power and authority from Satan (the dragon, v.11), and support from his allies to cause "the earth and them which dwell therein to "worship" the first beast" (Rev. 13:12), there would not be any reprimands or threats of retribution or sanctions upon his supporters; but, whenever things do not go his way, or some countries do not want to adhere to the 2nd beast, the 2nd beast will flex his muscles with threats and ultimatum to do as he says or else suffer the consequences.

Here is the reference.

> "₁₃ And he [2nd beast] doeth great wonders, so that he maketh fire come down from heaven on the earth in the sight of men" (Revelation

The 3 Angel's Messages – ***The Great Tribulation***

13:13).

Needless to say at this point, today, Britain and America (2nd beast) are the most powerful countries of the world. Their war machines, satellites, drones, lasers, proton bombs, microwave weapons, stealth, and the ability to fight a war, without an army, by sitting on an arm chair with a joy stick, the 2nd beast can bring fire from the sky on the insubordinate with deadly accuracy, and that should give you an idea how powerful the 2nd beast is. Nonetheless, Britain and America are also the most powerful countries in world trade, money markets, and the number of allies they have amassed. And, if a country does not play their game, they can isolate that country and bring it into poverty very quickly by the use of successive use of sanctions and other means, which he has at his disposal.

The 2nd beast _____ 1). He *"deceiveth them that dwell on the earth by The means of those miracles which he had power to do in the sight of the beast."* 2). *"saying to them that dwell on the earth, that they should make an image to the beast."*

The next literal evil act of the 2nd beast, during the "great tribulation," is to,

> "14 deceiveth them that dwell on the earth by the means of those miracles which he had power to do in the sight of the beast; saying to them that dwell on the earth, that they should make an image to the beast, which had the wound by a sword, and did live" (Revelation 13:14).

When the second beast came on the world scene, he appeared to the world as a gentle world power (horns like a

The 3 Angel's Messages – **The Great Tribulation**

lamb); but at the same time spoke with lies (v11). And as the 2nd beast began to grow into a world power, he began to realize that he could not win support from the world populous by the gun only; he had to win the hearts and minds of all of the religious communities of the world, in order to successfully control all of the world masses. That is the reason the 2nd beast (Britain & America) began to foster the world religions in their respective countries, persuade, and entice all of these religious communities to accept the 1st beast as their spiritual leader and eventually cause them to worship the 1st beast (Rev. 13:12). And, if they don't, the 2nd beast is going to flex his muscles politically and religiously (Rev. 13:13) and push the issue upon them, in order for them to acknowledge the 1st beast of Revelation 13:1-3 as their spiritual leader of all the world.

And as the kings and kingdoms of the world and the churches of the world gradually begin to acknowledge the 1st beast, as their spiritual leader, Satan and his evil angels will begin to work miracles through them, in order to stay the three angels messages, and claim to the world that the three angel's messages, of Revelation 14:6-11, are not of God.

But, the three angel's messages are unstoppable; by the power of God the Holy Spirit and in the name of Jesus Christ the LORD, thousands upon thousands begin to leave the 1st beast's churches. And thousands upon thousands begin to leave the Muslim churches, Jewish churches, Christian churches, Greek Orthodox church, and from other faiths, and embrace the three angel's messages. And in the name of Jesus Christ the LORD, and by the power of God the Holy Spirit, they push forward to finish the work on planet earth during the "great tribulation."

Seeing that the three angel's messages are unstoppable, and people are leaving the Muslim, Jewish, Christian, and other churches by the droves, Satan in desperation initiates a deceptive plan. And that deceptive plan is to deceive the

The 3 Angel's Messages – *The Great Tribulation*

people of the world by impersonating Christ's second coming. Thus, when Satan's commanding angels prepare Satan's evil angels to play their deceptive part and everyone is ready for Satan's grand entrance, Satan appears in the form of a brilliant light form before the public, here and there, throughout the world, healing people from their deceases, healing their broken limbs, restoring their eye sight, feeding the hungry, speaking words of wisdom, and claiming that he is Christ.

Day after day, Satan with his deceptive deprave evil acts continues to convince the deceived crowds who reject the warning from the followers of the three angel's messages that he cannot be Jesus Christ the LORD because Jesus Christ's second coming does not take place during the "great tribulation." And, Christ's second coming does not take place before the "sign" of Christ appears in heaven. Christ's second coming takes place after the "sign" of Christ appears in heaven. And, as per scripture, the "sign" of Christ appears right after the "great tribulation" and not before (Matthew 24:29, 30). And another reason why the appearance of those individuals who claim that they are Christ, cannot be Christ is simply because when Christ comes with His holy angels to planet earth, He is not going to step down on earth. Christ and His holy angels will remain visible way up in the sky for all to see (Revelation 1:7; Matthew 24:27).

In passing, let me make one very important point. Satan and his satanic agencies cannot produce or reproduce or copy or imitate, or duplicate the "sign" of Jesus Christ. For those reasons you will not see the "sign" of Christ visible in the sky before Satan tries to impersonate Christ's second coming, during Satan's impersonation of Christ's second coming, and after Satan's impersonation of Christ's second coming.

And the reason Satan and his satanic agencies will not imitate Christ's second coming after the "sign" of Christ appears after the "great tribulation," is due to the fact that after

The 3 Angel's Messages – ***The Great Tribulation***

the "sign" of Christ appears in heaven, Christ's decree will be uttered, which states;

> "₁₁ He that is unjust, let him be unjust still: and he which is filthy, let him be filthy still: and he that is righteous, let him be righteous still: and he that is holy, let him be holy still." Revelation 22:11

Once the above decree is uttered, God's people will be sealed, and there will be no more people who would want to be saved. And, once the above decree is uttered by Jesus Christ the LORD, there would not be any more people to be deceived. Therefore, it would not be profitable for Satan and his satanic agencies to impersonate Christ's second coming after the "sign" of Christ appears in heaven.

Therefore, when Satan impersonates Christ's second coming and attempts to convince the world that he is Christ, do not believe him. And, if others, who are devil possessed, appear and claim that they are Christ, or claim that they are prophets, Jesus said, "believe them not."

Irrespective how many miracles Satan and his admirers perform, before, during, and after Satan impersonates Christ's second coming, and how impressive and convincing Satan looks in his brilliant light form that he disguises himself in, we are warned regarding Satan's appearance and his ministers appearances;

> "₁₄ And no marvel; for Satan himself is transformed into an angel of light.

> "₁₅ Therefore it is no great thing if his ministers also be transformed as the ministers of righteousness; whose end shall be according to

The 3 Angel's Messages – **The Great Tribulation**

their works." 2 Corinthians 11:14, 15

And, here is Christ's warning to you and to me, regarding Satan's attempt and other's who will attempt to impersonate Christ's second coming, during the "great tribulation," which you and I are living in.

> "21 For then shall be great tribulation, such as was not since the beginning of the world to this time, no, nor ever shall be. 22 And except those days should be shortened, there should no flesh be saved: but for the elect's sake those days shall be shortened.
>
> "23 Then if any man shall say unto you, Lo, here is Christ, or there; believe it not. 24 For there shall arise false Christs, and false prophets, and shall shew great signs and wonders; insomuch that, if it were possible, they shall deceive the very elect.
>
> "25 Behold, I have told you before. 26 Wherefore if they shall say unto you, Behold, he is in the desert; go not forth: behold, he is in the secret chambers; believe it not. 27 For as the lightning cometh out of the east, and shineth even unto the west; so shall also the coming of the Son of man be.
>
> "28 For wheresoever the carcase is, there will the eagles be gathered together.
>
> "29 Immediately after the tribulation of those days shall the sun be darkened, and the moon shall not give her light, and the stars shall fall from heaven,

The 3 Angel's Messages – **The Great Tribulation**

and the powers of the heavens shall be shaken:

> "30 And then shall appear the sign of the Son of man in heaven:

> "and then shall all the tribes of the earth mourn, and they shall see the Son of man coming in the clouds of heaven with power and great glory." Matthew 24:21-30

A very adequate warning don't you think?

To avoid deception, we must meat all who confront us with misquoted scripture, opinions, and claims of who they are, by the words of the Gospel of Jesus Christ the LORD (Mark 1:1). Therefore listen to the words of Jesus Christ in the above verses (Matt. 24:21-30), and take heed not to be deceived as others who would not take heed to Christ's words are deceived and would be deceived; and perhaps be lost for eternity, if they do not change their minds.

Perhaps, you might be surprised to know that today, as you are reading this book, there are millions upon millions of people out there who knock on people's doors, claiming that Jesus Christ the LORD has already returned to planet earth and is dwelling in a secret place. How can anyone believe that claim is mind boggling, especially when Jesus has already warned by saying,

> "26 Wherefore if they shall say unto you, Behold, he is in the desert; go not forth: behold, he is in the secret chambers; believe it not." Matthew 24:26

Obviously, their claim cannot be true because they claim that Jesus came about 100 years ago! And that claim cannot be true because when Jesus returns the 2nd time, every eye will see Him (Revelation 1:7) because His visibility will be,

> "27 as the lightning cometh out of the east, and shineth even unto the west; so shall also the coming of the Son of man be." Matthew 24:27

The other reason why their claim, and others like them who claim that Jesus has already come, cannot be true is simply because Jesus 2nd coming is not going to take place before the "great tribulation" takes place. And another reason their claim is not true is simply because Christ's return does not take place during the "great tribulation." Furthermore, their claim is not true because Christ's return does not take place before the "sign" of Christ appears in heaven. Christ's 2nd coming takes place in heaven after the "sign" appears in heaven.

Therefore for anyone to claim that Christ is already here is deceived and is trying to deceive you. Be aware and take Christ's passionate warning as it is given in Matthew 24:21-30 and Revelation 1:7.

On the other hand, if Jesus Christ has already returned to earth 100 years ago, why is Satan impersonating Christ's 2nd coming during the "great tribulation"? That is a total contradiction between him and his representatives.

Nonetheless, seeing that Satan's impersonation of Christ's second coming is going to be successful to some degree, he stops his charade, and resorts to aggressive covert sadistic efforts to implement more miracles through the supporters of the 2nd beast's religious and political agenda, in order to convince the world masses that he, as Christ, has empowered those of the 2nd beast; and therefore making many of the public believe that he is Christ and their miracles are God sent.

The 3 Angel's Messages – **The Great Tribulation**

The 2nd beast ___ 1). *"had power to give life unto the image of the beast [1st beast]."* 2). *"and cause that as many as would not worship the image of the beast should be killed."*

And by deceiving the masses of the world "by the means of those miracles which he had power to do," the 2nd beast tells them to "make an image to the beast [1st beast, Rev. 13:1-3], which had the wound by a sword, and did live" (Revelation 13:14).

And in regards to the "image" of the first beast (papacy), it is the character, the pagan religious doctrine such as hell, purgatory, Sunday worship, priests, popes, Mary asking favors from Christ, idols, rosary, praying to dead people, Trinity, co-creator, priests forgiving sins, the outward appearance, the beliefs of the papacy and Vatican city, and what they stand for. Thus making an "image" to the papacy (1st beast) is a culmination of all the above attributes of what the pope stands for. And those of the 2nd beast who want to make an "image" to reflect the pope's attributes, it means that they want the pope to be their spiritual leader and adhere to his pagan religious doctrine. That is where the 2nd beast wants to lead his followers while they are in a state of deception.

But, at that time, of Revelation 13:14, as hard as Satan and his satanic agencies try to convince the masses of the world to join the 2nd beast's ranks, and make and image to the 1st beast, more people are convinced that those who present the three angel's messages are speaking the truth, and the 2nd beast and the pope are speaking lies and misleading people. Therefore, the more Satan and his satanic agencies, through the empowerment of the 2nd beast, try to stop converts going to Jesus Christ the LORD, the more keep accepting Jesus as their LORD God and Savior. And that infuriates Satan.

In his furry, Satan takes more drastic devious measures, in order to stop the flow of converts to Jesus Christ. He

The 3 Angel's Messages – **The Great Tribulation**

further empowers the 2nd beast to do his oppressive bidding. We are told:

> "15 And he [2nd beast] had power to give life unto the image of the beast [1st beast], that the image of the beast [1st beast] should both speak, and cause that as many as would not worship the image of the beast should be killed." Revelation 13:15

Now, the intimidation and brutal persecution, like the 1st beast before him, begins to take place more rigorously. The 2nd beast gives an ultimatum to the world that they should worship the "image" of the pope (predominately Sunday worship). And if they don't, a law is going to be implemented "that as many as would not worship the image of the beast [1st beast] should be killed." Revelation 13:15

Millions upon millions of religious and none religious men and women because their freedom of speech and freedom to worship has been taken away from them by the 2nd beast; they begin to listen to the three angels messages more intently and search more fervently the scriptures of the Bible and join the persecuted men and women who have made a stance with the believers of the three angel's messages.

Seeing that the nonconformists would not give up their stance in the three angel's messages, the second beast by the political and civil laws gathers as many of the nonconformists as he can into the prison camps. And, if that is not bad enough, the 2nd beast, like his predecessor (1st beast), tortures, beats, starves, and uses all manner of evil methods to make the nonconformist give up their faith in the three angel's messages. But the nonconformist cannot be swayed. They stand firm in the scriptures of the Bible and in the name of Jesus Christ their LORD, they continue to spread the three angel's messages

The 3 Angel's Messages – **The Great Tribulation**

even to their abusers.

But Satan, the 1st beast, and the second beast are not receptive to the three angels messages. Therefore they take the nonconformists before the public and kill many of them; in order to instill fear upon the on lookers, so that they would not join the cause of the nonconformists. But God's people are not deterred by the imprisonment, persecution, and killings of their fellow believers.

The *"warning of the second angel."*

Now because all of those churches and atheists who refuse to repent and have joined the ranks of the 2nd beast and are worshiping the 1st beast and are persecuting all who have accepted the three angel's messages, the warning of the second angel begins to resonate more fervently,

> "₈ saying, Babylon is fallen, is fallen, that great city, because she made all nations drink of the wine of the wrath of her fornication."
> Revelation 14:8

Of what "city" is Apostle John talking about in the above verse; and who or what is "Babylon"?

Conceder the following: The "little horn" (kingdom) that came out of the "ten horns" (kingdoms) and dethroned "three horns (kingdoms) in the vision of Daniel 7 are the same 10 horns in the vision, which Apostle John saw in Revelation 13:1-3. Therefore, the seven headed beast of Revelation 13:1-3, is also the beast with the seven heads and ten horns of Revelation 17:3 on which the "woman" is sitting upon.

Therefore, the "great whore that sitteth upon many waters" (Rev. 17:1) is the same "woman" that is seated upon a "scarlet coloured beast, full of names of blasphemy [See Rev.

13:2 also], having seven heads and ten horns" (v.3). "4 And the woman was arrayed in purple and scarlet colour, and decked with gold and precious stones and pearls, having a golden cup in her hand full of abominations and filthiness of her fornication:

> "5 And upon her forehead was a name written, MYSTERY, BABYLON THE GREAT, THE MOTHER OF HARLOTS AND ABOMINATIONS OF THE EARTH." Revelation 17:4, 5

As per verses four and five above, we are also told that the "woman" who was sitting upon the "scarlet coloured beast" is identified by the name of "Babylon."

So, who or what does the "woman" that is sitting upon the scarlet beast represent?

The answer is given. The prophet of the LORD says,

> "18 And the woman which thou sawest is that great city, which reigneth over the kings of the earth" (Revelation 17:18).

Therefore, the "woman" that is sitting upon the "beast" is identified by the name of "Babylon" "the mother of harlots" and as the "great city, which reigneth over the kings of the earth" (Revelation 17:18).

Where is this city located?

Again the answer is given. The "whore" is the "woman" (city) that "sitteth upon many waters" (Rev. 17:1).

What does "sitteth upon many waters" represent?

According to v.15, the "many waters" are explained. "And he saith unto me, The waters which thou sawest, where the whore sitteth, are peoples, and multitudes, and nations, and tongues" (Rev. 17:15). And as per v.15, the "woman" (city) is located in a very heavy populated area. But more precisely, as per v.9, the "seven heads" of the beast that the "woman" (city) is sitting on is located upon the seven mountains of Rome.

Here is the reference:

> "9 The seven heads are seven mountains, on which the woman [city, v.18] sitteth" (Revelation 17:9).

Thus, in reference to the papacy and their Vatican city, in Daniel 7 and in Revelation 13, after the removal of the pope in 1798 AD by Napoleon Bonaparte, the city and the popes, up until now, were represented without any serious status in the world stage. But, in Revelation 17, the pope and Vatican city are said to be sitting upon the top of the pinnacle. We are told, the "woman" (city, v.18), "1 that sitteth upon many waters," is the city "2 With whom the kings of the earth have committed fornication, and the inhabitants of the earth have been made drunk with the wine of her fornication. And the "many waters" that the woman (city) is sitting upon, "15 are peoples, and multitudes, and nations, and tongues" (Revelation 17:15).

Therefore, when power and authority is given to Vatican city by the 2nd beast, during the "great tribulation," Vatican city will be sitting on top of the summit; and she will be in control of the world affairs because the second beast (Britain & America) have given her the power to exercise her will. And her will, unfortunately, like the 2nd beast, is to eradicate anyone or anything that would stand in her way and prevent her to have full control of the world masses. Therefore, those who will not conform to her political and religious agenda, now that she is back in the driver's seat, her wrath is "full of abominations and filthiness of her fornication" and resentment towards the nonconformists. She wants to

The 3 Angel's Messages – ***The Great Tribulation***

wipe out of the face of the world all who attempt or toy with the idea of accepting the three angel's messages. Especially, towards the converts to the three angel's messages. Apostle John describes her venomous wrath this way; he says,

> "6 And I saw the woman [the city of Rev. 17:18] drunken with the blood of the saints, and with the blood of the martyrs of Jesus" (Revelation 17:6).

Therefore, as per the above verse, the "whore" that is identified as the "woman" who is sitting on top of "nations, kindreds and tongues" is that "18 great city, which reigneth over the kings of the earth" (Revelation 17:1, 18). She is further identified by the name of "Babylon the great," which is "drunken with the blood of the saints, and with the blood of the martyrs of Jesus" (Revelation 17:5, 6).

The fact that the "woman" (city) and her "harlots" that support her are "drunken with the blood of the saints, and with the blood of the martyrs of Jesus," during the "great tribulation," it sends a strong signal to the dwellers upon the earth and upon the second angel of the LORD that "Babylon" and her "harlots" have fallen into total apostasy by not repenting for their evil acts, and have chosen to continue with their onslaught to persecute and kill God's people; and therefore, that acknowledgment is heralded by the second angel of the LORD,

> "8 saying, Babylon is fallen, is fallen, that great city, because she made all nations drink of the wine of the wrath of her fornication."
> Revelation 14:8

The 2nd beast _____ *"causeth all,…to receive a mark in their right* hand, or in their foreheads."

The next abominable and inhumane evil act to take place, during the "great tribulation," is the enforcement, by the 2nd beast, upon all the people of the world to receive a "mark" in the forehead or in the "right hand."

Here is the reference:

> "16 And he [2nd beast] causeth all, both small and great, rich and poor, free and bond, to receive a mark in their right hand, or in their foreheads" (Revelation 13:16).

Seeing that the death penalty of Revelation 13:15 does not stop or deter the masses of the world to convert to the three angel's messages, and accept Jesus Christ as their LORD God and Savior, Satan becomes even more furious with his evil angels and with the 2nd beast because they failed and are failing to deceive and to stop the effectiveness of the three angel's messages; but more so with all of the converts to the three angel's messages and with the rest of the nonconformist.

Therefore, Satan by the use of the 2nd beast and the 1st beast, implements all of the depraved sanctions that he can upon all of the people of the world who do not conform to his political and religious dictates, via the insertion of a tracking device, called "mark," that is inserted "in their foreheads" or in their "right hand," in order to further discourage people from accepting the three angel's messages and from accepting Jesus as their LORD God and Savior.

This tracking device, which is inserted in your "forehead" or in your "right hand"— if you allow them— is also identified by the "name of the beast," or by the "number of his name." Revelation 13:17

Here is the reference:

The 3 Angel's Messages – **The Great Tribulation**

> "17 And that no man might buy or sell, save he that had the mark, or the name of the beast, or the number of his name" (Revelation 13:17).

In regards to tracking devices as you have read in the above verse, one type of a tracking device is identified as "the mark," and the other tracking device is identified by "the name of the beast" (pope), the other tracking device is identified by the "number of his name" (pope). I state that the "number of his name" refers to the pope because we are told that the number 666 "**is the number of a man.**" And, when you add the numbers from the pope's Latin name, you will come up with the total that will equal to 666.

Here is the reference:

> "18 Here is wisdom. Let him that hath understanding count the number of the beast: for it is the number of a man; and his number is Six hundred threescore and six" (Revelation 13:18).

Did you notice, we are told in the above verse that the "the number of the beast" is "the number of a man" (Revelation 13:18). And we are also told, "his number is Six hundred threescore and six [666]" (Revelation 13:18).

The man's name (pope) in Latin, according to John Joseph McVey, we are told,

> "The pope is the vicar of Christ, the successor of St. Peter, and the visible head of the Church." * 5

***** 5 *Manual of Christian Doctrine,* John Joseph McVey, 1914, p.123

The 3 Angel's Messages – **The Great Tribulation**

Although the Vatican and its popes can claim all they want that they are the "vicar's" of Christ, it does not make them so because Apostle Peter never claimed that he is the "vicar" of Christ and neither any of the other apostles make that claim. Therefore for anyone to claim that they are the "vicar" of Christ is an outright blasphemy and an abomination to Jesus Christ the LORD. It should be noted: Jesus did not appoint a "vicar," a high priest, or any priest in the New Testament. And the reason Christ did not appoint vicars or high priests is due to the fact that the Old Testament ceremonial law and its services were abolished on Calvary's cross by Jesus Christ the Lamb who taketh away the sins of the world.

So! Since Christ abolished the Leviticall priesthood, why would anybody go against Christ's will and defiantly institute the priesthood in their church. Especially when their priests are not descendants from the tribe of Levi?

Here is the reference:

> "15 Having abolished in his flesh the enmity, even the law of commandments contained in ordinances; for to make in himself of twain one new man, so making peace" (Ephesians 2:15).

Therefore, as per the above verse and other like verses, since the ceremonial law, which contained the services of the Levitecall priesthood, burnt offerings in the eastern courtyard of the Sanctuary, and the sprinkling of the animal's blood have been done away on Calvary's cross, the Roman Catholic church falsely misrepresents Jesus Christ the LORD by implementing priests in its church and is falsely claiming that the popes have been appointed as "vicar's" of Christ the LORD. There is not a single reference in the entire Bible to support their claims.

Nonetheless, since the pope still claims that he is the

The 3 Angel's Messages – ***The Great Tribulation***

"vicar" of Christ, and as per scripture (Bible), he can never be; but because he does not want to relinquish that claim, here is his Latin name, which is printed on his hat, and the calculation of his name.

His name in Latin is: VICARIUS FILII DEI.

The calculation is as follows:

V = 5	F = 0	D = 500	
I = 1	I = 1	E = 0	Total = 112
C = 100	L = 50	I = 1	53
A = 0	I = I	501	501
R = 0	I = 1		666
I = 1	53		
U = 5			
S = 0			
112			

As you can see from the above calculation, the number of the man's name is 666 (Rev. 13:17). And the man with the number 666, is identified first as the 1st beast of Revelation 13:1-3. And then, he is identified as "a scarlet coloured beast" (Rev. 17:3). And this beast of Revelation 17:3 is further identified as the eighth king who subdued three kings out of the ten kings and is part of the seven kings (Rev. 17:11). And this beast (1st beast of Rev. 13:1-3) has a name whose number is 666.

And this man (pope), with his newly found friend (the 2nd beast), has a special tracking devise for you that can give the pope a real time status of your body vitals, what you do, where you go, with whom you interact and say, and whether you are alive or not.

The Sign in Matthew 24 *By: Philip Mitanidis* _____ 109
The 3 Angel's Messages – **The Great Tribulation**

When you cannot "buy or sell."

    If you refuse to accept the "mark" (tracking device) in your "forehead" or in your "right hand," as millions upon millions will refuse, you will not be able to "buy or sell" commodities, have a bank account, health card, driver's license, rent, buy food, buy milk for the baby, clothing, go to school, work, etc., etc. If you refuse to receive the tracking device, you will become a man, a woman, or a child without a country. You will be a fugitive sought after by the authorities world wide and branded as a criminal of the state and of your country.

    Stop and think for few moments and consider one of the resent most devastating typhoons ever recorded in the history of the world that hit the Philippines early in November 2013, and headed to Vietnam. The devastation upon human life, homes, buildings, roads, vehicles, hydro plants, food factories, transportation, communication devices, etc., etc., by typhoon "Haiya" left the living stranded and nowhere to go for help. And when some trucks with food tried to go to the needy, gangs took the food in order to repackage and sell it in the market place for large profit. And even worse, people found themselves robed from their possessions and from the little food they had left. Thousands upon thousands were left homeless, no place to go, no place to sleep, no food, no water, no electricity, no medicine, no blankets, no warm clothing, no transportation, no gas, no telephone service, no toilets, no soap to wash with, no sanitary facilities, no help for the helpless such as little children that were separated from their parents. And no help for the elderly who could not sustain themselves, no help for the sick, and those that were not turned away, only got first aid help because there was no hospitals and doctors and nurse's to attend to them, nowhere to wash and clean their bodies, no means to wash with and clean their clothes, no access to their money, neither were people able to buy the essentials because there weren't any to buy, and the list of woes of affliction, and desperation surmounted into unbearable conditions of survival.

On a positive note, the people in the Philippines were not persecuted, burnt to the stake, hanged from the gallous, killed at will, forced into prison camps, tortured, and their properties confiscated from them. They were free to move about and go wherever they wanted in order to solve their problems.

On the other hand, now consider even the more inhumane and oppressive conditions the people of God and the nonconformists to the 2nd beast and to the 1st beast are going to be put through, by simply refusing to accept their tracking devices and become their enslaved drones.

There would be no comparison to what degree of pain and agony God's people would be going through during and near the end of the "great tribulation" because the wicked will put on the evil character of Satan; therefore their evil acts will be imposed upon God's people and upon others as far as their imagination can **take them.**

> Jesus said, "37 But as the days of Noe [Noah] were, so shall also the coming of the Son of man be." Matthew 24:37

So! How wicked was the imagination of the unrepentant sinner during Noe's days?

Here is the answer:

> "5 And GOD saw that the wickedness of man was great in the earth, and that every imagination of the thoughts of his heart was only evil continually." Genesis 6:5

The 3 Angel's Messages – **The Great Tribulation**

According to the above verse the thoughts of the wicked antediluvians, during Noah's time, were "only evil continually." And because "every imagination of the thoughts of his heart was only evil continually," Jesus Christ the LORD added,

> "22 except those days should be shortened, there should no flesh be saved: but for the elect's sake those days shall be shortened." Matthew 24:22

The severity of the persecution and not being able to buy, even the necessities of life for survival, compels Jesus to say, "except those days should be shortened, there should no flesh be saved: but for the elect's sake those days shall be shortened."

Thank the LORD for His promise that "those days should be shortened,…for the elect's sake"; and for the fact that they are not going to be tempted beyond what they are able to bear (1 Corinthians 10:13).

At that time, men and women will not be able to buy or sell unless they have a tracking device inserted in their "right hand" or in their "forehead." But, since God's people and other nonconformists are going to refuse to be branded as slaves and supporters of the 1st beast and of the 2nd beast's abominable, oppressive, and offensive political and religious policies, they are going to find themselves homeless, with no food, no water, no toilets, no clothing, no blankets, no cell phones, no jobs, no homes, no cars, no work, no doctors, no hospital to take care of them, etc., etc., and on top of all that, they would be fugitives in their own countries sought after by the local and international evil authorities.

And even worse, God's people at that time will be betrayed by their brothers, sisters, mothers, fathers, grand

The 3 Angel's Messages – ***The Great Tribulation***

parents, relatives, so called friends, strangers, and so on.

So! Under those brutal and inhumane conditions, where can God's people go to escape the authorities and survive their adversaries?

Well, I do not know about you; but as far as I am concerned, the first place I would go to is under the wings of Christ my LORD God and Savior and stay there until I am sealed for eternal life, no matter what the consequences might be.

The final warning _____ by the third angel's message, to a perishing world, during the "great tribulation," but more fervently during the implants of the tracking devices.

While the 1st beast and the 2nd beast insert their tracking devices throughout the world to willing hands and to the deceived masses, the third angel of the LORD of hosts is going to herald its message more passionately by willing hands, to a perishing world saying;

> "9 with a loud voice, If any man worship the beast and his image, and receive his mark in his forehead, or in his hand, 10 The same shall drink of the wine of the wrath of God, which is poured out without mixture into the cup of his indignation; and he shall be tormented with fire and brimstone in the presence of the holy angels, and in the presence of the Lamb [Christ]: 11 And the smoke of their torment ascendeth up for ever and ever: and they have no rest day nor night, who worship the beast and his image, and whosoever receiveth the mark of his name." Revelation 14:9-11

The last call to repentance and salvation by the third

The 3 Angel's Messages – **The Great Tribulation**

angel's message above is self-explanatory; and therefore we do not have to go into a lot of detail. The third angel says with a loud voice, "If any man worship the beast [1st beast] and his image [religious doctrine], and receive his mark in his forehead, or in his hand [tracking devices], 10 The same shall drink of the wine of the wrath of God, which is poured out without mixture [without mercy upon the wicked] into the cup of his indignation;

"10 and he shall be tormented with fire and brimstone in the presence of the holy angels, and in the presence of the Lamb [Jesus Christ the LORD]:

"11 And the smoke of their torment ascendeth up for ever and ever: and they have no rest day nor night, who worship the beast and his image, and whosoever receiveth the mark of his name." Revelation 14:9-11

Needless to say, this final warning of the third angel's message is similar to the time when the Antediluvians saw the last event take place, during the procession, when the holy angels brought the animals, birds, reptiles, and made them enter Noah's ark (boat). This event took place just before Jesus Christ the LORD closed the boat's side door. And once the door was closed no man, women, or child was able to go in the boat. Probation had closed. All who refused to go into the ark were left out to suffer the consequences. In fact, Jesus warned as to how callous and proud people were and are going to be before He comes the second time to take His people to their heavenly home.

> Jesus said, "37 But as the days of Noe [Noah] were, so shall also the coming of the Son of man be. 38 For as in the days that were before the flood they were eating and drinking, marrying and giving in marriage, until the day that Noe entered into the ark, 39 And knew not until the

flood came, and took them all away; so shall also the coming of the Son of man be.

"40 Then shall two be in the field; the one shall be taken, and the other left. 41 Two women shall be grinding at the mill; the one shall be taken, and the other left.

"42 Watch therefore: for ye know not what hour your Lord doth come. 43 But know this, that if the goodman of the house had known in what watch the thief would come, he would have watched, and would not have suffered his house to be broken up.

"44 Therefore be ye also ready: for in such an hour as ye think not the Son of man cometh." Matthew 24:37-44

But, you and I do not have to be like the Antediluvians; we are given plenty of prophetic sequential events in the eight verses of the "great tribulation" (Revelation 13:11-18) and Matthew 24:29, 30 for us to follow. And by watching these prophetic events taking place and unfold before our eyes, we can know how close Christ's second coming is going to be. And since we are living at the beginning of verse twelve, of Revelation thirteen, you can very easily follow each prophetic event from one verse to the next.

In fact, if you want, you can even memorize each prophetic event of the "great tribulation" starting from v.11 and right up to verse eighteen so that you can identify each event when you hear about it or when you see it happen. That way you will be in the know and alert of all the events that have

The 3 Angel's Messages – ***The Great Tribulation***

taken place and the next event that is going to take place. And when the last event of the "great tribulation" takes place, you will be ready to watch for the awesome and devastating events that will follow the "great tribulation" before the "sign" of Christ takes place in the heaven. I make that statement because Jesus Christ the LORD said,

> "29 Immediately after the tribulation of those days shall the sun be darkened, and the moon shall not give her light, and the stars shall fall from heaven, and the powers of the heavens shall be shaken:
>
> "30 And then shall appear the **sign** of the Son of man in heaven: and then shall all the tribes of the earth mourn, and they shall see the Son of man coming in the clouds of heaven with power and great glory." Matthew 24:29, 30

In closing, here are the literal sequential events of the "great tribulation" that effect you personally.

> "11 And I beheld another beast coming up out of the earth; and he had two horns like a lamb, and he spake as a dragon.
>
> "12 And he exerciseth all the power of the first beast before him, and causeth the earth and them which dwell therein to worship the first beast, whose deadly wound was healed.
>
> "13 And he doeth great wonders, so that he maketh fire come down from heaven on the earth in the sight of men,

"₁₄ And deceiveth them that dwell on the earth by the means of those miracles which he had power to do in the sight of the beast; saying to them that dwell on the earth, that they should make an image to the beast, which had the wound by a sword, and did live.

"₁₅ And he had power to give life unto the image of the beast, that the image of the beast should both speak, and cause that as many as would not worship the image of the beast should be killed. "₁₆ And he causeth all, both small and great, rich and poor, free and bond, to receive a mark in their right hand, or in their foreheads:

"₁₇ And that no man might buy or sell, save he that had the mark, or the name of the beast, or the number of his name.

"₁₈ Here is wisdom. Let him that hath understanding count the number of the beast: for it is the number of a man; and his number is Six hundred threescore and six." Revelation 13:11-18

~~~

"₂₀ He [Christ the LORD], which testifieth these things saith, Surely I come quickly. Amen. Even so, come, LORD Jesus.

"₂₁ The grace of our LORD Jesus Christ be with you all. Amen." Revelation 22:20, 21

The "Sign" of Christ

The "Sign" of Christ

So! Of what "sign" is Jesus Christ the LORD of hosts talking about in Matthew 24:30?

If you were to read Matthew 24, you would notice that four apostles asked Jesus privately three questions. They said,

> "3 Tell us, when shall these things be? and what shall be the sign of Thy [Your] coming, and of the end of the world?" Matthew 24:3

The first question they asked Jesus was to tell them "when shall these things be?" This question was in reference to the "sign" that would reveal the destruction of Jerusalem and the Sanctuary.

The second question that was posed to Jesus by the apostles was in regards to the "sign" that would warn the world of the nearness of His second coming. They asked, "what shall be the sign of Thy [Your] coming"?

And the third question they asked was in regards to the end of the world; they said, "and of the end of the world?" Matthew 24:3

The "Sign" of Christ

The answer to the first question to John, James, Peter, and Andrew was answered by Apostle Luke during the time he wrote the Gospel according to Luke; see Luke 21:20. But, Apostle John, Apostle Mark, and Apostle Matthew do not give us an answer or even mention the "sign" in their Gospels, regarding the "sign," which would warn the residents of Jerusalem that the destruction of their city is imminent, as we have studied before. But, in regards to the two last questions, Jesus lumped them together when He gave the apostles an answer. Jesus said,

> "29 Immediately after the tribulation of those days shall the sun be darkened, and the moon shall not give her light, and the stars shall fall from heaven, and the powers of the heavens shall be shaken:
>
> "30 And then shall appear the sign of the Son of man in heaven: and then shall all the tribes of the earth mourn, and they shall see the Son of man coming in the clouds of heaven with power and great glory.
>
> "31 And he shall send his angels with a great sound of a trumpet, and they shall gather together his elect from the four winds, from one end of heaven to the other." Matthew 24:29-31

Did you notice?

In the above verses, Jesus gives an answer to the apostles that a "sign" would appear in heaven after "the powers of the heavens shall be shaken" (v.29). But, Jesus does not describe "the sign" (v.30).

The "Sign" of Christ

And in regards to their question of the end of the world, Jesus places that event after "30 the tribes of the earth mourn" (Matthew 24:30). And after "the tribes of the earth mourn," "30 they shall see the Son of man [Christ] coming in the clouds of heaven with power and great glory.

31 And He shall send his angels with a great sound of a trumpet, and they shall gather together His elect from the four winds, from one end of heaven to the other." Matthew 24:29-31

In passing, let me make clear one point for you in regards to Christ's second coming. Although Jesus states that His visible 2nd coming will take place after the "sign" of the Son of man (Christ) appears in heaven, for all to see, and "all the tribes of the earth mourn," when they see it; He leaves few details as to what transpires between the appearance of the "sign" in heaven and His 2nd coming.

Here are few events of many that are going to take place between the "sign" appearing in heaven and Christ's second coming.

After the "sign of the Son of man [Christ]" appears in heaven, the judgment upon God's people will be terminated. And after the judgment is over, the decree of Revelation 22:11 will be uttered,

> "11 He that is unjust, let him be unjust still: and he which is filthy, let him be filthy still: and he that is righteous, let him be righteous still: and he that is holy, let him be holy still." Revelation 22:11

After the decree is uttered, Christ's penitent people, wherever they would be on planet earth, at that time, they will be sealed as His sons and daughters, and be ready for Christ's 2nd coming to take place. And after God's people are sealed in

The "Sign" of Christ

their forehead by the holy angel's of Jesus Christ the LORD, there will be few more gripping human tragedies and heart breaking events taking place before the seven last plagues of Revelation 16 begin to fall upon the unsaved and upon the ecosystem of the earth. It should be noted that the plagues are for the wicked and not for the redeemed. The plagues will fall upon the unsaved (Revelation 18:4) before Christ's second coming takes place "with power and great glory."

Therefore because of these scriptural facts, we can conclude that the second coming of Christ the LORD of hosts does not take place right after the "sign of the Son of man [Christ]" appears in heaven for all to see. It takes place near the end of the seven last plagues of Revelation sixteen.

And, during that time, the holy angels will "$_{31}$ gather together His [Christ's] elect from the four winds, from one end of heaven to the other" (Matthew 24:31). Jesus and the holy angels with the redeemed will leave behind planet earth with all of the wicked, and head for the third heaven. And, as they leave, the last plague of Revelation sixteen, which contains hail weighing about 60 lbs each, will fall upon planet earth and upon the wicked. The prophet of the LORD adds,

> "$_{17}$ Fear, and the pit, and the snare, are upon thee, O inhabitant of the earth. $_{18}$ And it shall come to pass, that he who fleeth from the noise of the fear shall fall into the pit; and he that cometh up out of the midst of the pit shall be taken in the snare: for the windows from on high are open, and the foundations of the earth do shake.
>
> "$_{19}$ The earth is utterly broken down, the earth is clean dissolved, the earth is moved exceedingly. $_{20}$ The earth shall reel to and fro

By: Philip Mitanidis

The "Sign" of Christ

like a drunkard, and shall be removed like a cottage; and the transgression thereof shall be heavy upon it; and it shall fall, and not rise again." Isaiah 24:17-20

As you have read above, the condition of planet earth is very bleak, gloomy, and destructive. We are given a glimpse of what the end of the world looks like in the above verses. The conditions that are described of the earth, by the prophet of the LORD, will be unbearable and unsustainable for life forms, as we know them, when planet earth "shall reel to and fro like a drunkard" in the cold, cold, dark space of the universe.

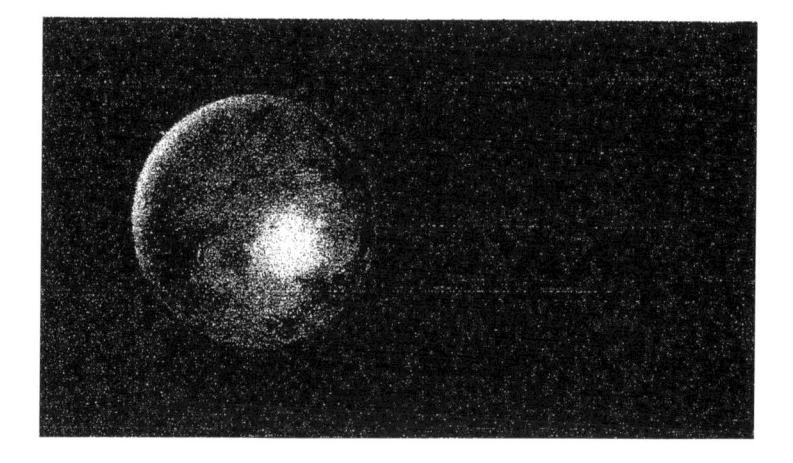

Although Jesus gives the apostles an answer in regards as to when the end of the world will take place, and after what event, but, in regards to the "sign," Jesus does not give them an answer as to what the "sign of the Son of man [Christ]" looks like, or describe the "sign." He simply says that a "sign" will appear in heaven after "the powers of the heavens shall be shaken" (v.29).

The "Sign" of Christ

And the other clue that was given to the four apostles was the time period the "sign" would appear, where, and after what sequential events it would take place.

Jesus said,

"29 Immediately after the tribulation of those days shall the sun be darkened, and the moon shall not give her light, and the stars shall fall from heaven, and the powers of the heavens shall be shaken:

"30 And then shall appear the sign of the Son of man in heaven: and then shall all the tribes of the earth mourn, and they shall see the Son of man coming in the clouds of heaven with power and great glory. 31 And he shall send his angels with a great sound of a trumpet, and they shall gather together his elect from the four winds, from one end of heaven to the other." Matthew 24:29-31

So! When was the "sign" of the Son of man [Christ]" going to take place, after what event, and where?

Here are the answers:

When _____ was the "sign" of the Son of man [Christ]" going to take place? According to Jesus statement, in the above verses, the "sign" of Christ was going to take place "immediately" after "the tribulation" (v.29).

After what event _____ was the "sign" of the Son of man [Christ]" going to take place? According to the above verses, it will take place after "the powers of the heavens shall be shaken" (v.29).

The "Sign" of Christ

Where _____ was the "sign" of the Son of man [Christ]" going to take place? According to v.30, it will appear in the entire "heaven" because the scrolling of the heaven means that the heaven as we know it now, with all of its planetary systems, will not be there! Revelation 6:14

To further clarify the above verses, of Matthew 24:29-31, here is an overview in a sequential point form of the events, which Jesus is talking about.

> First event that would take place "immediately after the great tribulation," is the literal darkening of the "sun."
> Second event that would take place, which would be affected by the darkening of the sun, is the moon. The "moon shall not give her light."
> Third event after the Moon does not give her light is the falling of the stars "from heaven."
> Fourth event after the stars fall from heaven, will be when "the powers of the heavens shall be shaken:"
> Fifth event after the heavens are shaken, the appearance of the "sign of the Son of man [Christ]" takes place in heaven. But, as you have observed, there is nothing in the above verses to tell us what the "sign" is and what it looks like. All we are told is simply that it would appear in heaven after the powers of heavens are shaken. That's it!
> Sixth event that is going to take place after the "sign of the Son of man Christ]" appears heaven, is the event when "all the tribes of the earth mourn." They "mourn" because they see Christ's literal "sign" in heaven, which confirms

The "Sign" of Christ

> the fact that Christ's 2nd coming is soon to take place "30 with power and great glory." Matthew 24:30
>
> Seventh event that is going to take place after "all the tribes of the earth mourn," according to Matthew 24:30, is Christ's second coming with "power and great glory." And after Christ comes, the end of the world will take place (Isaiah 24:17-20).

As you have already noticed in the above verses, Apostle Matthew does not give to us a description of the "sign" of the Son of man (Christ); he simply says that a sign will appear in heaven after the "tribulation." Therefore in order to get an answer regarding the description of the "sign," we can go to Apostle Mark's Gospel and review his presentation of the "sign" of the Son of man (Christ) and see the outcome.

Apostle Mark writes,

> "24. But in those days, after that tribulation, the sun shall be darkened, and the moon shall not give her light, 25 And the stars of heaven shall fall, and the powers that are in heaven shall be shaken.
>
> "26 And then shall they see the Son of man coming in the clouds with great power and glory. 27 And then shall he send his angels, and shall gather together his elect from the four winds, from the uttermost part of the earth to the uttermost part of heaven." Mark 13:24-27

As you have noticed, verse twenty-four and v.25 of Mark 13 is almost word for word with Mathew's presentation

The "Sign" of Christ

in Matthew 24:29. But when you read Mark 13:26 and compare the verse to Matthew 24:30, you will notice that there is a different presentation by Apostle Mark. Mark makes a very short comment. He says,

> "26 And then shall they see the Son of man coming in the clouds with great power and glory." Mark 13:24-27

Apostle Mark in verse twenty-six avoids mentioning the "sign" of the Son of man (Christ) appearing in heaven, where it will appear, and after what event? Where as Apostle Matthew states that the "sign of the Son of man (Christ) appears in heaven (v.30), after the powers of heaven are shaken. And after the "sign" of Christ appears in heaven and the ungodly see it, "30 all the tribes of the earth mourn" (Matt. 24:30) because they know that Christ's second coming is soon to take place and they have nowhere to hide.

Therefore when you compare Mark's presentation to Matthew's presentation, you will notice Mark does not even mention the "sign" of the Son of man (Christ) appearing in heaven, where it will appear, or what it looks like. He goes directly to the time period when Christ returns for the second time with all of His angels with power and great glory to take His people away from this wretched, detestable, sin infested, human suffering, and cruel degenerate world of ours to their heavenly home where sin does not exist.

Apostle Luke, on the other hand, gives us more information and clarification on the status of the unsaved, and planet earth, in his presentation of the Gospel of Jesus Christ the LORD of hosts. He writes,

> "25 And there shall be signs in the sun, and in the moon, and in the stars; and upon the earth

The "Sign" of Christ

> distress of nations, with perplexity; the sea and the waves roaring;
>
> "26 Men's hearts failing them for fear, and for looking after those things which are coming on the earth: for the powers of heaven shall be shaken.
>
> "27 And then shall they see the Son of man coming in a cloud with power and great glory. 28 And when these things begin to come to pass, then look up, and lift up your heads; for your redemption draweth nigh." Luke 21:25-28

As you have noticed, Apostle Luke does not mention the "great tribulation" as his two contemporaries do (Matthew & Mark). He begins his narrative by saying, "25 And there shall be signs in the sun, and in the moon, and in the stars." But, he does not reveal what the "sun" is going to do or what the moon is going to do; instead, he reveals what kind of reaction the people of the world will have when they see these events taking place in heaven. He says that there will be "25 upon the earth distress of nations, with perplexity."

And then he reveals how the earth is going to react. He says "25 the sea and the waves roaring."

After that short introduction to the reaction of the sea, Luke returns to the reaction of the people of the world again and says, "26 Men's hearts failing them for fear, and for looking after those things which are coming on the earth: for the powers of heaven shall be shaken." Luke 21:25, 26

Apostle Luke reveals and concludes, as Mark did and as Matthew did, by saying, "for the powers of heaven shall be shaken."

But Apostle Luke, like Apostle Mark, avoids

The "Sign" of Christ

mentioning the "sign" of the Son of man (Christ) appearing in heaven. They both go directly to the time when Christ returns for the second time to planet earth.

He says,

> "27 And then shall they see the Son of man coming in a cloud with power and great glory." Luke 21:27

In his conclusion Luke adds,

> "28 And when these things begin to come to pass [what he wrote in these verses], then look up, and lift up your heads; for your redemption draweth nigh." Luke 21:25-28

As you can readily see, thus far, none of the three apostles reveal, explain, or describe the "sign" of the Son of man (Christ). All we know about the "sign," according to Matthew, is the fact that it will appear in heaven after the "powers of heaven" are "shaken." And when the wicked of the earth see the "sign" in heaven, they will "mourn" because they realize that the 2nd coming of Christ is soon to take place; and the time has come to face the consequences according to their evil works.

So! What about Apostle John, what does he say about the "sign" of Christ appearing in heaven?

Surprisingly, the Gospel according to Apostle John, does not reveal, describe, or even talk about the "sign" of the destruction of Jerusalem; or give to us a narrative, which describes or reveals the "sign" of the Son of man (Christ) appearing in heaven after the powers of heaven are shaken?

So! Why talk about a "sign" and avoid describing it?

Are we to guess what the "sign" looks like?

The "Sign" of Christ

That is not the case; we are told by Apostle Matthew that the wicked, when they see the "sign" of the Son of man (Christ) appear in heaven, they will recognize the "sign" and know what it means. And because the wicked recognize the "sign" and know what it means, when they see the "sign," they will "mourn" or greave if you like? That means that there is a description of the "sign" of the Son of man (Christ) somewhere in the Bible; but, as you have noted, the description does not exist in the four Gospels!

The avoidance of the description of the "sign" of Christ, for some or for many people, kind of begs the question; why is the description not in the Gospels? And why did Jesus, at that time, avoid giving to the apostles the description of the "sign" of His coming?

Simplistically, just like the other prophesies, the time for the revelation of the "sign" was not intended to be known prior to a set time of which God the Father has set for its revelation.

We are told,

> "1 God, who at sundry times and in divers manners spake in time past unto the fathers by the prophets, 2 Hath in these last days spoken unto us by his Son, whom he hath appointed heir of all things, by whom also he made the worlds." Hebrews 1:1, 2

If you look at the last part of the sentence in verse two above, you will notice that the Old King James Version of the Bible (OKJV) states,

> "by whom also he made the worlds"
> (Hebrews 1:2).

The "Sign" of Christ

The above statement cannot be true because there is no verse or verses in the entire sixty-six books of the Bible, which state that God the Father created something through Jesus Christ the LORD. Therefore the last part of the verse in Hebrews 1:2 cannot be true. And another reason why the statement in Hebrews 1:2 cannot be true in the OKJV of the Bible is due to the fact that the Greek text disputes it.

The Greek text reads,

"δι'   ου   εκαμε   και τους αιωνας."   Εβραιους 1:2
"by whom also he made the   worlds."   Hebrews 1:2

Did you notice the last English word "worlds" in the above verse of Hebrews 1:2?

And did you notice the last Greek word "αιωνας" in the above verse of Εβραιους 1:2 (Hebrews 1:2)?

That Greek word ("αιωνας") in English means "times" or "ages" if you like?

Therefore what the apostle is saying in Hebrews 1:2 is simply that God the Father has set up the "times" and the events to take place according to His wishes. And this same thought is presented to us in the book of Daniel.

The angel of the LORD of hosts said to Daniel,

"9 Go thy way, Daniel: for the words are closed up and sealed till the time of the end." Daniel 12:9

Conversely, Apostle John was told, in reference to the book of Revelation,

"10 And he saith unto me, Seal not the sayings of the prophecy of this book: for the time is at hand." Revelation 22:10

The "Sign" of Christ

Did you notice; the angel of the LORD said to Apostle John "Seal not the sayings...for the time is at hand." Revelation 22:10

Consequently, according to the above verses, we can conclude that the "time" to reveal the "sign of the Son of man [Christ] in heaven" was not at hand during the writing of the four Gospels. The "sign" had to be revealed in another time period; and so it is today, the "sign" of the Son of man (Christ) is revealed for you and for me and for the whole world in order to know what it looks like, where it will appear, after what sequential event, and what it means.

> Jesus said, "30 And then shall appear the sign of the Son of man in heaven: and then shall all the tribes of the earth mourn." Matthew 24:30

So! According to the above verse, "all the tribes of the earth" will "mourn" when they see the "sign" of the Son of man (Christ) appear in heaven. That means, all of the people of the world will know what the "sign" looks like, where it will appear, and what it means.

In order to find out what the "sign" of the Son of man (Christ) looks like, when it will appear, and where it will appear; first, consider the prophetic events according to Apostle Matthew and Apostle John that will take place before the "sign" of the Son of man (Christ) appears in heaven:

Here are the literal sequential prophetic events according to Apostle Matthew that will take place before the "sign" of the Son of man (Christ) appears in heaven to warn the people of planet earth that Christ's 2nd coming is soon to take place.

Jesus said,

> "29 Immediately after the tribulation of those

The "Sign" of Christ

days shall the sun be darkened, and the moon shall not give her light, and the stars shall fall from heaven, and the powers of the heavens shall be shaken:" Matthew 24:29

Here are the five points taken from the above verse of Matthew 24:29.

1). "Immediately after the tribulation"
2). "shall the sun be darkened"
3). "the moon shall not give her light"
4). "the stars shall fall from heaven"
5). "and the powers of the heavens shall be shaken:"

In comparison, now consider the prophetic events Apostle John describes in Revelation 6:12, 13 before the "sign" of the Son of man (Christ) appears in heaven to warn the world that Christ's 2nd coming is just around the corner.

"12 And I beheld when he [Christ] had opened the sixth seal, and, lo, there was a great earthquake; and the sun became black as sackcloth of hair, and the moon became as blood; 13 And the stars of heaven fell unto the earth, even as a fig tree casteth her untimely figs, when she is shaken of a mighty wind." Revelation 6:12, 13

And, here are the five points taken from the above verses of Revelation 6:12, 13 after the "sixth seal was opened."

1). "there was a great earthquake"
2). "the sun became black as sackcloth of hair"

The "Sign" of Christ

    3). "the moon became as blood"
    4). "the stars of heaven fell unto the earth"
    5). "when she is shaken of a mighty wind"

Did you notice the five points (1-5) in Matthew 24:29 in comparison to the five points (1-5) Apostle John makes in Revelation 6:12, 13? They are almost word for word the same. The only difference is point number one. Matthew states, "immediately after the tribulation," where as Apostle John says, "there was a great earthquake."

Therefore we can conclude that "immediately after the tribulation," 1), there is going to be "a great earthquake," 2) "the sun became black as sackcloth of hair," 3) "the moon became as blood," 4) "And the stars of heaven fell unto the earth," 5) and "when she is shaken of a mighty wind."

Now, let us consider the verses of Matthew 24:30, 31 and compare those verses to Apostle John's presentation in Revelation 6:14-17. And please notice, Matthew makes a reference to the "sign" of Christ in Matthew 24:30; and how Apostle John gives the description of the "sign" of Christ in Revelation 6:14.

Matthew writes, **"30 And then shall appear the sign of the Son of man in heaven:**

"and then shall all the tribes of the earth mourn, and they shall see the Son of man coming in the clouds of heaven with power and great glory. 31 And He shall send his angels with a great sound of a trumpet, and they shall gather together his elect from the four winds, from one end of heaven to the other." Matthew 24:30, 31

The "Sign" of Christ

Here are five points (6-10) taken from the above verses of Matthew 24:30, 31

6). "$_{30}$ **then shall appear the sign of the Son of man in heaven (v. 30)**"

7). "and then shall all the tribes of the earth mourn"

8). "and they shall see the Son of man coming in the clouds of heaven with power and great glory"

9). "$_{31}$ And He shall send his angels with a great sound of a trumpet"

10). "$_{31}$ and they shall gather together his elect from the four winds, from one end of heaven to the other"

And here is Apostle John's presentation in Revelation 6:14-17 of the same events; which includes the description of the "sign" of the Son of man (Christ), and where it will appear.

Apostle John writes,

"$_{14}$ **And the heaven departed as a scroll when it is rolled together;**

"and every mountain and island were moved out of their places.

"$_{15}$ And the kings of the earth, and the great men, and the rich men, and the chief captains, and the mighty men, and every bondman, and every free man, hid themselves in the dens and in the rocks of the mountains;

The "Sign" of Christ

> "16 And said [Greek text, say] to the mountains and rocks, Fall on us, and hide us from the face of him that sitteth on the throne, and from the wrath of the Lamb:
>
> "17 For the great day of His wrath is come; and who shall be able to stand?" Revelation 6:12-17

Here are the six points (6-11) taken from the above verses of Revelation 6:12-17

6). "**14 And the heaven departed as a scroll when it is rolled together**" **(v.14).**

7). "and every mountain and island were moved out of their places"

8). "And the kings of the earth, and the great men, and the rich men, and the chief captains, and the mighty men, and every bondman, and every free man, hid themselves in the dens and in the rocks of the mountains"

9). "And said [Greek text, say] to the mountains and rocks, Fall on us, and hide us from the face of him that sitteth on the throne"

10). "and from the wrath of the Lamb [Christ]":

11). "who shall be able to stand?"

So! According to the above references, Apostle Matthew refers to the "sign" of Christ in point number 6) by saying,

> "**30 then shall appear the sign of the Son of man in heaven**" **(Matt. 24:30).**

And Apostle John describes what the "sign" of Christ

The "Sign" of Christ

looks like in point number 6) by saying,

> "**14 And the heaven departed as a scroll when it is rolled together**" **(Revelation 6:14).**

Let me say again, Apostle Matthew in point number 6) (Matt. 24:30) refers to the "sign" of Christ appearing in heaven, after the "powers of the heavens shall be shaken," but, fails to illustrate or describe the "sign" in his presentation.

On the other hand, as you have read in Revelation 6:14, Apostle John not only refers to the "sign" of Jesus Christ the LORD, but at the same time he tells us where it will appear and how much of the heaven the "sign" of Christ the LORD of hosts is going to occupy. In addition, Apostle John also takes the time to describes what the "sign" of Christ looks like, in point number six, by saying to us.

> "**14 And the heaven departed as a scroll when it is rolled together**" **(Revelation 6:14).**

Did you notice the extraordinary scale of the "sign" of Jesus Christ the LORD?

We are told, the "sign" of Jesus Christ will occupy the whole heaven!

Let me say that again; we are told that the "sign" of Jesus Christ the LORD of hosts will occupy the whole heaven! And when it does, it will blanket the whole heaven. You can look up, down, north, south, east, west, and you will notice that every star, nebula, galaxy, black hole, mega suns, planets, etc., etc., will not be there. Heaven will be empty. And the reason this phenomenon will occur is to simply notify the world that probation of sinful living will soon be terminated and the second coming of Jesus Christ the LORD is just around the corner.

The "Sign" of Christ

Nonetheless, here is the description of the "sign" of Christ as it is presented to us by Apostle John, in Revelation 6:14, in a pictorial form. (See front cover also.)

The "Sign" of Christ

As you can see in the above illustration, the description of the "sign" of Christ is when you are looking at the teeming populated heaven with stars, suns, planets, galaxies, nebulae, black holes, etc., etc., all of the sudden, these heavenly bodies depart **"14 as a scroll when it is rolled together" (Revelation 6:14)** right before your eyes. And when that happens, you will know that event is the "sign" of Jesus Christ Apostle John is describing and talking about in Revelation 6:14; and Apostle Matthew is referring to in Matthew. 24:30.

And after all of these heavenly bodies **depart "as a scroll when it is rolled together,"** heaven will be void of its contents. Heaven will be empty. People will not be able to see what they were accustomed seeing before "the heaven departs as a scroll." The scientists will look and look with their scientific electronic gadgetry for these heavenly bodies, but to their surprise and dismay, they will not be able to find them! They will wonder with horror, dismay, and anticipation of the unknown coming events. And further wonder and ask, how can the universe all of the sudden be empty from its contents (planetary systems)?

They will wonder and ask, if our solar system broke away from the gravitational pull of our nearest galaxy?

They would ask, was planet earth flung off course or pushed somehow to the furthest remote corners of the universe? If so, is the earth capable of sustaining itself in a precise distance from the sun: and if it is, for how long?

Are we all alone in the empty universe?

And, since the planetary systems have disappeared, is planet earth next in line to vanish?

Will the universe return to normal again?

If the universe does not return to normal again, is planet earth going to remain displaced somewhere in the dark cold space of the universe or move elsewhere forever?

And they will wonder if the prophetic presentation of

The "Sign" of Christ

the "sign" of Christ, by Jesus Christ and Apostle John, is going to come to pass as they have stated in Matthew 24:29, 30 and Revelation 6:12-17?

But, the scientific community will not be alone with never-ending questions. When the news reporters around the world pick up on the event, they are going to have a field day with the scientific community, when they ask the scientists question after question. By not being able to give a logical and rational explanation to the news media, the scientists will fuel the worrisome minds of the people around the globe. Needless to say, at that time, they will receive unsatisfactory opinionated answers; but they cannot escape the fact that they recognize the meaning of the "sign" because they were told over and over again of these events, during the "great tribulation," when they were persecuting God's people, and the other nonconformists, by the political and religious oppressive arm of the 2nd beast.

Therefore because they know the meaning of the "sign," they shudder with anxiety, horror, and hate in the foreknowledge of the coming events; but more horrifying, knowing that the awesome bloodcurdling plagues are soon to fall upon them. And then, even more terrifying thoughts would come to mind; and that is, when the wicked see Jesus Christ the LORD of hosts coming back as LORD God and Savior to the Redeemed; He will appear as consuming terror to the defiant unrepentant evil men and women who scoffed and ridiculed and imprisoned and killed at will His people.

Nonetheless, to better understand the subsequent events, and between what two events the "sign" of Jesus Christ is tucked in, let me put the sequential events of Apostle Matthew and Apostle John side by side so that you can follow these events more easily, and get a better view of the order these events will occur.

Please note the accuracy of the two apostle's presentations; they are almost the same word for word.

The "Sign" of Christ

Matt. 24:29, 30	Revelation 6:12-17
1). "Immediately after the tribulation"	1). "there was a great earthquake"
2). "shall the sun darkened"	2). "the sun became black as sackcloth of hair"
3). "the moon shall not give her light"	3). "the moon became as blood"
4). "the stars shall fall from heaven"	4). "the stars of heaven fell unto the earth"
5). "and the powers of the heavens shall be shaken"	5). "when she is shaken of a mighty wind"
6). **"then shall appear the sign of the Son of man in heaven"**	6). **"And the heaven departed as a scroll when it is rolled together" (v.14).**
	7). "and every mountain and island were moved out of their places"
7). "and then shall all the tribes of the earth mourn"	8). "And the kings of the earth and the great men, and the rich men, and the chief captains, and the mighty men, and every bondman, and every free men, hid themselves in the dens and in the rocks of the Mountains."
8). "and they shall see the Son of man coming in the clouds of heaven with power and great glory"	
9). "And He shall send His angels with a great sound of a trumpet"	9). "And said [Gr. say] to the mountains and rocks, Fall on us, and hide us from the face of him that sitteth on the throne."
10). "and they shall gather together His elect from the four winds, from one end of heaven to the other"	10). "and from the wrath of the Lamb {Christ]."
	11). "who shall be able to stand?"

The "Sign" of Christ

It is quite obvious from the previous page, by looking at each point of what Apostle Matthew has written, and by comparing his writings to what Apostle John has written in the book of Revelation, you can readily see where the "sign" of Christ is located, described, and between what two points (events) it is wedged in. Therefore there is no question what all of the people of the earth will eventually see clearly and vividly in heaven. And, it should be noted; this prophetic event, the scrolling of the heaven, just like the previous events, they are all literal and humongous events. They cannot be missed! And the reason why they cannot be missed is due to the fact that when these events appear, one after another, they will linger for a while so that even the people in the most remote and secluded areas of the world would not be able to miss them.

The eleven points that are mentioned by Apostles Matthew and John are literal and aptly described for you and for me, just as the prophetic events of the "great tribulation" (Rev. 13:11-18) are aptly described and are literal events that are taking place, today, while you are reading this book. Therefore, you should be concerned when somebody tells you that these events are not literal.

Why would anyone say that the "great tribulation" is literal and not the "sign" of Christ and the rest of the points that are mentioned by Apostle Matthew and by Apostle John? Is it because Apostle John reveals and describes the "sign" of Christ in the book of Revelation?

If that is the case, why accept the "great tribulation" of Revelation 13:11-18 as being literal and say, Revelation 6:12-17 is figurative?

That does not make any sense?

Did you know that the majority of the prophetic events, in the book of Revelation, are literal?

Check them out?

Furthermore, why do some people disagree with the

The "Sign" of Christ

sequential events of Matthew 24:29-31 and Revelation 6:12-17 as they are presented to us by the apostles?

Do people really think that Jesus Christ the LORD of hosts did not know what order to put these events in?

If so! You must know that these literal sequential events are not going to go away any time soon? Especially when they are coming right at you in power and majesty.

In fact, as time goes on, they will become even more revealing so that you can follow each event and know what the next event is going to be; that is how literal these events are going to be — they are worldwide events. You will not be able to mistake them when you are in the thick of them. And right now, you are in the thick of the events that are described in Revelation 13:12. The mentors of the second beast (Britain & America) whether you know it or not, are forging forward with their insane evil plans to control you and the world masses, in order to bring the population down to a handful of people for manageability purposes and to make them become their slaves.

You can pooh, pooh the above remarks all you like; but, you are already part of the "great tribulation." You are living at the beginning of Revelation 13:12. And the next literal event of Revelation 13:12 is in progress. You can follow the events of the "great tribulation" as they were itemized for you previously; and as they appear in their sequential form in Revelation 13:11-18 for your consideration. And, as it was stated before, the last event of the "great tribulation" was going to take place when the implants of the tracking devices in the "right hand" or in the "forehead" are forced upon the people by law. And if you reject that law and the implants of the tracking devices, you will not be able to buy or sell commodities. And after the implants, homelessness, persecution, overflowing prison camps, and countless of fugitives and deaths, we are told that there is an end to the "great tribulation."

The "Sign" of Christ

Jesus said,

"₂₉ Immediately after the tribulation of those days shall the sun be darkened, and the moon shall not give her light, and the stars shall..." (Matthew 24:29)...

And after the "great tribulation," the following literal sequential events will take place:
Jesus said,

1). *The "great tribulation"* _____ Did you notice? Jesus said, "₂₉ Immediately after the tribulation of those days" (Rev. 13:11-18), certain events were to take place. The word "after" in the above quotation means "immediately" following the "tribulation" something was going to take place.

2). *There was "a great earthquake"* _____ And in this case, according to Matthew, we are told, "shall the sun be darkened." But, prior to the "sun be darkened," according to Apostle John, 1) there is going to be "a great earthquake" (Revelation 6:12). And when this mega-earthquake takes place, the minds of the people of the world will shift from the implants and persecution of the nonconformists to the humongous devastation of the "great earthquake."

If the mega-earthquake of which Apostle John is talking about occurs on land, especially in a heavily populated area, the toll of the suffering could very well be in the millions. The dead bodies under the rubble of building and heavy debris will not be reached on time, as we have seen historically. Their bodies will begin to stink and decompose causing air born diseases to spread throughout the area and beyond. The millions of traumatized wounded would be in pain. Human misery will abound, not only from their physical pain and

The "Sign" of Christ

agony, but also from their emotional state of mind. They would be in shock from looking at the magnitude of destruction and of the loss of human life. The wounded will also be suffering from air borne gas, methane, electrical fallout, dust, no toilets, no food, no clean water, no blankets, no shelters, no protection from the elements, no protection from thieves, and the list will go on and on.

But, if a mega-earthquake occurs way out in the sea, it will first draw the attention of the people of the world; and when they see the mammoth tsunamis forming and heading towards the land, they will issue warnings to ships and coastal areas, in order to save lives and minimize the destruction and the death toll it would cause.

But, if the mega-earthquake took place in the ocean, near land, the destruction of towns, cities, and life forms would be even more horrendous. And then, the search for the dead, wounded, crippled, and survivors will begin. And unfortunately, human misery, and desperation will grip the devastating areas. The human anxiety, pain, and the human emotion to find their loved ones, dead or alive, will cause an untold misery and agony. The need to find and to bury the dead by the survivors, the need for medical care, food, water, shelter, and protection from animals, looters, bullies, infectious diseases, and so on, will weaken the survivors into jeopardy, if they are not reached in time.

3). *And "the sun became black as sackcloth of hair"*___

And while the authorities, volunteers, news media, survivors, and the people of the world try to help rebuild the devastated communities, the next literal event inline will take place and cause the people of the world to look up into the heavens. And that next event, according to Matthew is when, 2) "the sun" shall "be darkened" (Matthew 24:29). And according to John, 2) "the sun became black as sackcloth of

The "Sign" of Christ

hair" (Revelation 6:12).

Can you imagine what the people of the world and the scientific communities would be thinking, when they see "the sun became black as sackcloth of hair"?

Most of the people of the world would be perplexed; and the words in the coffee shops and in the work place unending. But the spin-doctors of the news media and clergy will direct the people to think in terms of whatever untruths they feed them, or cling to the opinions of their friends. But the scientists would wonder what caused the sun to be darkened? How is it going to affect the earth's temperature? And, if the temperature falls below freezing or worse, how is the world food going to be produced? How are plants and trees going to survive or reproduce? Will there be sufficient oxygen reproduced by the remaining vegetation for the human race to breath? And the situation would be even more urgent because under the circumstances, how is the human race going to survive, if the freezing temperatures are prolonged; the energy supplies will dwindle, clean water will become scarce, and food supplies will continue to diminish?

4). *The "moon became as blood"* _____ And on top of the uncertainty, perplexity will set in, and emotional anxiety will spread throughout the world, while the people of the world scramble for answers and how to survive. And while the masses of planet earth look upon the sun darkened, during the day, they will also see the unnatural appearance of the moon. According to Matthew, 3) "the moon shall not give her light" (Matthew 24:29). And according to apostle John, 3) "the moon became as blood" (Revelation 6:12). This event also worries the masses of the earth and wonder what is happening to the sun? Is it going to stop shining? Is it going to implode or explode? And, if it does, will the moon loose its orbit and collide with the earth? Or will the earth and the moon be

The "Sign" of Christ

sucked into the sun? Fear sets into people's minds of the things they see taking place, and worry of the unknown outcome of the moon, and of the earth, and of the sun. Bewilderment and confusion sets in throughout the world because the scientists cannot give the people concrete answers. And because their politicians and their religious leaders are telling people lies in order to pacify them; but the events, which they see and experience tell them that these events are there to warn that life on planet earth will soon be over, even though they do not want to accept that outcome.

     5). *The "stars of heaven fell unto the earth"* _____ And while the politicians and their mentors, scientists, and religions that bow down to the first beast, pray to their gods for a good outcome, the next event is ready to follow, which is, according to Matthew, 4) "the stars shall fall from heaven" (Matthew 24:29). And according to John, 4) "And the stars of heaven fell unto the earth" (Revelation 6:13).

Historically, we had meteor showers fall upon the earth before; but, what about now? How intense and devastating are these meteors going to be?

According to Matthew's and John's statements, direct hits by meteors will fall upon the earth. But how brutal the impact would be will depend how large the meteor is going to be after part of it is burnt up by the earth's atmosphere? But much of the debris is going to be very severe because both apostles state that 5) "the powers of the heavens shall be shaken" (Matthew 24:29). And again, 5) "even as a fig tree casteth her untimely figs, when she is shaken of a mighty wind" (Revelation 6:13).

Although much of the world scientists are working today very hard to produce equipment that would deflect or destroy the meteors coming towards planet earth, as you have read, prophetically, according to Apostle John, 4) "the stars of

The "Sign" of Christ

heaven fell unto the earth" (Revelation 6:13).

Therefore the destruction of property, lakes, rivers, trees, animals, human life, and so on will continue to take its toll as the earth rotates around the sun. And as the earth rotates, the human eye will continue to focus upon the events that are taking place in the sky and wonder, what horrifying event is coming upon them next. But, God's people will not wonder what is coming next, they know what the coming events are and wait patiently for them to come and pass.

6). And *"then shall appear the sign of the Son of man in heaven"* _____But the wicked are not ignorant; they were told of the coming events; and therefore, they are not in the dark about these events. They just hoped that these events did not come to pass. Then again, many of the wicked thought that Christ would not allow the destruction to take place because they thought that the destructive forces would also destroy God's people. Therefore, the wicked thought that they too would be safe. Of course Christ will protect His people during those coming events. The only difference between the wicked and God's people is the fact that the wicked chose not to be protected, by rejecting salvation, and not repenting for their evil acts. They prefer to live in sin. But as far as the coming events are concerned, the wicked are more than knowledgeable about the itemized events. In fact, when they see the "sign" of Christ in heaven, their reaction tells us that they recognize it and know what are the sequential events, and what they signify.

Therefore, when the people of planet earth see the "sign" of Christ (6th event) appear in heaven, — as Apostle Matthew refers to it,

> "30 **And then shall appear the sign of the Son of man in heaven" Matthew 24:30.**

The "Sign" of Christ

And, as Apostle John describes the "sign," so eloquently in the following manner,

> "14 **And the heaven departed as a scroll when it is rolled together**" Revelation 6:14,

—in acknowledgment that Christ's 2nd coming is around the corner, "30 then shall all the tribes of the earth mourn" (Matthew 24:30).

They mourn because the wicked know and tremble at the thought of the coming deadly and horrifying events. And yet, they still choose to live in sin.

> "7 Wherefore do the wicked live, become old, yea, are mighty in power? 8 Their seed is established in their sight with them, and their offspring before their eyes.

> "11 They send forth their little ones like a flock, and their children dance. 12 They take the timbrel and harp, and rejoice at the sound of the organ. 13 They spend their days in wealth, and in a moment go down to the grave.

> "14 Therefore they say unto God, Depart from us; for we desire not the knowledge of thy [Your] ways."

The "Sign" of Christ

> "11 And for this cause God shall send them strong delusion, that they should believe a lie: 12 That they all might be damned who believed not the truth, but had pleasure in unrighteousness." Job 21:7, 8, 11-14; 2 Thessalonians 2:11, 12

And, as the wicked look towards heaven, ponder, and tremble in fear at the "sign of Christ's 2nd coming," the next overwhelming event, after the "sign," takes place.

7). *We are told, "every mountain and island were moved out of their places"* _____ While the people of planet earth are gazing at the "sign" of Christ in heaven, and wondering how did all of the planetary systems vanish from space; on earth, "every mountain and island were moved out of their places" (Revelation 6:14).

Can you comprehend what the statement denotes when it says, "every mountain" is moved out of its place?

If you do, now picture the size of the mountain that is near by you and what it would take to move it out of its place? Can you imagine how humongous the energy level has to be in order to move one mountain out of its place? And even more awesome is the fact that you not only need enormous energy to move the mountain but at the same time, you need energy to move the mountain in one direction or another, for some distance, against other resistant rocks, soil, trees, or mountains.

And that is not the end of the apostle's statement. He says, "every mountain" were "moved out of their places." If you have a picture of the humongous energy that would take for one mountain to move out of its place, now multiply that amount by the number of mountains that are throughout the world and it will give you an idea how great the energy source has to be in order to move every mountain out of their places.

But the prophet of the LORD of hosts does not end

The "Sign" of Christ

his statement there; he also adds, and every "island were moved out of their places."

Although the energy to move every mountain out of their places would be considerable greater than the energy to move all of the islands out of their places because the ocean water is less resistant to the movement of land mass, this energy that is needed to move the islands out of their places also goes off the charts.

And when you take the time to combine the energy that would take for all of the mountains and for all of the islands to be moved out of their places, personally, I cannot visualize the mega energy without the use of some supper computer to analyze and tally up the figures for me.

But, even if I am unable to fully comprehend the unending zero's after a number, the amount of energy that is needed to move "every mountain and island…out of their places," I am appalled at the enormous devastation of loss of life, pain, agony, tears, anxiety, strife, homeless, hunger, destitute, suicide rate, chaos, etc., etc., that is going to grip the whole world when the mountains and the islands move out of their places.

By considering the above events, can you comprehend how many world-wide living souls are going to be lost or dislodged or loose their homes because of the land shift and loss of islands?

And when the land in the various continents shifts away or into another sovereign country, will the territorial borders be settled peaceably or will they be settled with war?

And we can even ask, will the land on which buildings and homes once stood, be settled peaceably or violently? And how will the land disputes be settled where some land lots will disappear and some land lots will enlarge and some land lots will encroach upon other land lots, and so on?

And what would happen to all who have survived and

The "Sign" of Christ

are displaced, especially those who have lost islands on which their land once stood? Would other countries, at that time, take them in or would they be left and identified as fugitives without a country?

Should I go on?

In any case, it is not a good picture.

Although I still fail to fully comprehend the immense world wide spread of destruction that is going to take place, this much I do know; by "every mountain and island" being "moved out of their places," it will cause the earth to tremble, infrastructure to break, earthquakes to take place, the oceans to roar, the tsunamis to swell and swallow everything in their paths. Human life and animals will be perplexed, terrified, and not knowing what to do. They will seek help from others to only find out that others are in the same perplexed and fearful and helpless state of mind.

And when that happens, those two combined events— the "sign" and the removal of mountains and islands out of place— will create even greater fear, dismay, and havoc in the hearts and minds of the men, women, and children of the earth.

The prophet of the LORD says,

> "25 upon the earth distress of nations, with perplexity; the sea and the waves roaring; 26 Men's hearts failing them for fear, and for looking after those things which are coming on the earth" (Luke 21:25, 26).

According to the prophet of the LORD, the people of planet earth will be in shock, dismay, anxiety, their hearts failing from fear, and in a state of vulnerability, while they look upon the events that are coming their way. And these events will not get any better? They are even worse than the previous ones.

8). *And say to "the mountains and rocks, Fall on us,"* _____

The "Sign" of Christ

_____ Failure to find consolation, the wicked begin to emulate other human beings who throughout the world think that the second coming of Christ is at hand; and therefore these people join the prominent people, such as the kings of the earth, great men and women, rich men and women, bondmen, bondwomen, free men and women, the chief captains, and so on, seeking shelter in the dens, in the silos, in the mountains, and wherever else they could hide.

Here is the reference.

> "14 and every mountain and island were moved out of their places. 15 And the kings of the earth, and the great men, and the rich men, and the chief captains, and the mighty men, and every bondman, and every free man, hid themselves in the dens and in the rocks of the mountains; 16 And said [Greek text, say] to the mountains and rocks, Fall on us, and hide us from the face of him that sitteth on the throne, and from the wrath of the Lamb [Christ]: 17 For the great day of His wrath is come; and who shall be able to stand?" Revelation 6:14-17

Did you notice?

All of these mighty men and women who thought that they are untouchable and unmovable and defiant to Christ and to His authority; now are saying to the mountains and to the rocks, "16 Fall on us, and hide us from the face of him that sitteth on the throne, and from the wrath of the Lamb [Christ]" Revelation 6:16

Did you observe; these mighty men and women, "said [Greek text, say] to the mountains and rocks, Fall on us, and hide us"? Did you also notice that the wicked men and women are asking the rocks and mountains not to kill them; they are

The "Sign" of Christ

asking them to hide them. In other words, they want to continue to live in sin and not in righteousness. In fact many of the wicked, after they see the "sign" of Christ in heaven, and survive the plagues, they continue to do evil works.

Here are the references:

> "$_{20}$ And the rest of the men which were not killed by these plagues yet repented not of the works of their hands, that they should not worship devils, and idols of gold, and silver, and brass, and stone, and of wood: which neither can see, nor hear, nor walk:
>
> "$_{21}$ Neither repented they of their murders, nor of their sorceries, nor of their fornication, nor of their thefts." Revelation 9:20, 21

As you can readily observe in the above verses, the wicked men and women do not want to repent and be saved in Christ's kingdom because in Christ kingdom sin does not exist there. They would not be happy there. But, if the wicked wanted to live in righteousness, they would be looking for Christ's second coming with great desire and admiration.

Instead, they are asking the mountains and the rocks to hide them from God the Father and from God the Christ [Lamb].

For how long?

Preferable forever, but deep down in their hearts, they know that the time of retribution is at hand.

9). *Thee 2nd coming is at hand.* _____ They know that the 2nd coming is at hand because they say,

> "$_{17}$ For the great day of His [Christ] wrath is

The "Sign" of Christ

come; and who shall be able to stand?" Revelation 6:17

Finally, the arrogant wicked people, who persecuted Christ the LORD through His people, acknowledge that no one can stand up against Christ the LORD of hosts. He is what He claimed all along. He is the God of His universe; and nobody can remove Him from His throne. Satan tried by himself in heaven and failed. Satan and his evil angels jointly tried in heaven and failed. Satan tried again all by himself to deceive Christ in the wilderness, when Christ began His ministry (Matthew 4:1-11). Again Satan, his evil angels, and wicked men and women, who worship Satan, tried to remove Christ from His throne when He came to planet earth, in the flesh, to pay for the sins of the repentant sinners, and failed miserably. So, now, while Christ has put on His power and majesty, "[17] who shall be able to stand?" (Revelation 6:17). Obviously no one is able to stand against Christ; or capable of dethroning Christ from His lofty throne; and the wicked recognize that fact. And by recognizing that fact, they know deep down in their hearts that they cannot escape His wrath.

But, to the repentant sinners, who are abused by the wicked, jailed, starved, beaten, ridiculed, tormented, and made them outcasts and fugitives in their own countries, Christ the LORD of hosts has come to deliver them from their evil persecutors, who found joy in their torment.

At that time, when Christ returns for the second time to planet earth with "power and great glory," and with His holy angels, we are told,

"[7] every eye shall see Him" (Revelation 1:7).

And He will see every eye that is looking at Him. There would be nowhere for the wicked to hide.

The "Sign" of Christ

But, before we stand in the presence of Christ the LORD of hosts during His 2nd coming, before we are told to worship the 1st beast, before the death penalty is issued, before we are told to worship the image of the 1st beast, before the implants of the "mark" of the beast are inserted in the people's right hands or in their foreheads, before the great earthquake takes place, before the sun becomes dark, before the moon becomes like blood, before the stars of heaven start to fall upon the earth, before the powers of heaven are shaken, preferably before the "sign" of Christ is revealed in heaven, before "every mountain and island were moved out of their places," and before the decree of Revelation 22:11 is uttered, my prayer for the people of the world is that they would choose Jesus Christ as their LORD God and Savior; and when they find themselves standing before Christ, at His second coming, they would rejoice and receive eternal life in Christ's kingdom, where happiness and contentment abound.

And if you choose to accept Jesus Christ as your LORD God and Savior, today, remember, "immediately" after the great tribulation," there is going to be a "great earthquake," and after that event,

> "25 there shall be signs in the sun, and in the moon, and in the stars; and upon the earth distress of nations, with perplexity; the sea and the waves roaring; 26 Men's hearts failing them for fear, and for looking after those things which are coming on the earth: for the powers of heaven shall be shaken.

> "27 And then shall they see the Son of man coming in a cloud with power and great glory.

> "28 And when these things begin to come to

The "Sign" of Christ

pass, then look up, and lift up your heads; for your redemption draweth nigh." Luke 21:25-28

Meanwhile, welcome back to the "great tribulation."

These final prophetic events that were written 2,000 years ago are upon us. You and I are living in the time period of Revelation 13:11, and at the beginning of Revelation 13:12, and waiting for the "sign" of Christ to appear in heaven to let us know that His second coming is just around the corner.

~~~

"21 The grace of our LORD Jesus Christ be with you all. Amen." Revelation 22:21

THE SIGN

APPENDIX

Here are the sequential events of the "great tribulation" and of "the sign" of Jesus Christ the LORD.

Sequence | Revelation 13:11-18

1). "11 And I beheld another beast coming up out of the earth; and he had two horns like a lamb, and he spake as a dragon.
2). "12 And he exerciseth all the power of the first beast before him,
3). "and causeth the earth and them which dwell therein to worship the first beast, whose deadly wound was healed.
4). "13 And he doeth great wonders, so that he maketh fire come down from heaven on the earth in the sight of men,
5). "14 And deceiveth them that dwell on the earth by the means of those miracles which he had **power to do in** the sight of the beast;
6). "saying to them that dwell on the earth, that they should make an image to the beast, which had the wound by a sword, and did live.
7). "15 And he had power to give life unto the image of the beast,
8). "that the image of the beast should both speak, and cause that as many as would not worship the image of the beast should be killed.
9). "16 And he causeth all, both small and great, rich and poor, free and bond, to receive a mark in their right hand, or in their foreheads:
10). "17 And that no man might buy or sell, save he that had the mark, or the name of the beast, or the number of his name.

11). "₁₈ Here is wisdom. Let him that hath understanding count the number of the beast: for it is the number of a man; and his number is Six hundred threescore and six" (Revelation 13:11-18)

Sequence   Matthew 24:29-31
12). "₂₉ Immediately after the tribulation" event number
13). thirteen takes place ("₁₂ there was a great earthquake." Revelation 6:12)
14). "₂₉ of those days shall the sun be darkened,
15). "₂₉ and the moon shall not give her light,
16). "₂₉ and the stars shall fall from heaven,
17). "₂₉ and the powers of the heavens shall be shaken:
18). "**₃₀ And then shall appear the sign of the Son of man in heaven:** ("₁₄ And the heaven departed as a scroll when it is rolled together;" Revelation 6:14).
19). ("₁₄ and every mountain and island were moved out of their places." Revelation 6:14)
20). "₃₀ and then shall all the tribes of the earth mourn," ("₁₅ And the kings of the earth, and the great men, and the rich men, and the chief captains, and the mighty men, and every bondman, and every free man, hid themselves in the dens and in the rocks of the mountains;" Revelation 6:15).
21). "₃₀ and they shall see the Son of man coming in the clouds of heaven with power and great glory." ("₁₆ And said [Gr. say] to the mountains and rocks, Fall on us, and hide us from the face of him that sitteth on the throne, and from the wrath of the Lamb. ₁₇ For the great day of his wrath is come; and who shall be able to stand?" Revelation 6:16, 17).
22). "₃₁ And He shall send his angels with a great sound of a trumpet, and they shall gather together his elect from the four winds, from one end of heaven to the other" (Matthew 24:31).

End of sequence

Revelation 6:12-17 complements Matthew 24:29-31; and at the same time, it describes the "sign" of which Jesus is referring to in Matthew 24:30

13). "12 And I beheld when he had opened the sixth seal, and, lo, there was a great earthquake;
14). "12 and the sun became black as sackcloth of hair,
15). "12 and the moon became as blood;
16). "13 And the stars of heaven fell unto the earth,
17). "13 even as a fig tree casteth her untimely figs, when she is shaken of a mighty wind.
18). ("30 And then shall appear the sign of the Son of man in heaven:" Matthew 24:30) **"14 And the heaven departed as a scroll when it is rolled together;**
19). "14 and every mountain and island were moved out of their places.
20). "15 And the kings of the earth, and the great men, and the rich men, and the chief captains, and the mighty men, and every bondman, and every free man, hid themselves in the dens and in the rocks of the mountains;" ("30 and then shall all the tribes of the earth mourn," Matthew 24:30).
21). "16 And said [Gr. say] to the mountains and rocks, Fall on us, and hide us from the face of him that sitteth on the throne, and from the wrath of the Lamb: "17 For the great day of his wrath is come; and who shall be able to stand?" ("30 and they shall see the Son of man coming in the clouds of heaven with power and great glory. 31 And He shall send his angels with a great sound of a trumpet, and they shall gather together his elect from the four winds, from one end of heaven to the other" Matthew 24:30,31).

QUESTIONS

1). How many disciples spoke to Jesus privately, regarding the destruction of Jerusalem?
2), What three questions did the disciples ask Jesus?
3). How many of the three questions did Jesus answer?
4). Describe the "sign," which revealed that the destruction of Jerusalem and the Sanctuary were imminent.
5). Who only describes the "sign" that would alert the destruction of Jerusalem?
6). What general and armed forces destroyed Jerusalem and the temple, after Jesus was crucified?
7). In what year was the Temple and Jerusalem destroyed?
8). What was the name of the Roman general that destroyed Jerusalem?
9). What did the Roman general do with the survivors of Jerusalem?
10). Who rebuilt Jerusalem and the Temple?
11). Why was Jerusalem attacked again?
12). Who attacked Jerusalem again?
13). What year did the siege take place?
14). Why did the surviving Jews flee Palestine?
15). What decree was made against the Jewish nation?
16). What god did the Romans place in the Temple of Jerusalem?
17). What year were the Jews allowed to return to Palestine?
18). To whom did the English government give the Sanctuary that is in Jerusalem?
19). Why do you think the British gave half of the

Questions

Sanctuary to the Jews and the other half to the Muslims?
20). Are the Jews still God's people today?
21). If you answered "Yes" or "No," give an explanation?
22). Is the Gospel of Jesus Christ the LORD of hosts preached today?
23). Why is the LORD sending three angels to planet earth to preach their respective messages?
24). a) How many messages is the first angel preaching?
b) Name the three messages.
25). What are the second and third angel's messages?
26). In what book and chapter of the Bible do we find the "great tribulation"?
27). What are the literal sequential events of the "great tribulation"?
28). Who or what is the first beast of Revelation 13?
29). Who or what is the second beast of Revelation 13?
30). What man has the number 666?
31). Why will the 1st & 2nd bests make it mandatory to insert tracking devices to all of the human beings?
32). Into what part of the human body are the tracking devices inserted?
33). How many tracking devices will they use?
34). Once the tracking device is inserted in a person, whose property does that person become?
35). Why would a person not be able to buy or sell commodities?
36). What will happen to the nonconformists who would not conform to the political and religious dictates of the 1st beast and to the 2nd beast.
37). What or who is Babylon of Revelation 17?
38). Who or what is the woman that is sitting on top of the beast in Revelation 17?

The Sign in Matthew 24 *By: Philip Mitanidis*

Questions

39). What do many waters represent in Revelation 17?
40). What is Babylon going to do to Christ's penitent people?
41). Who are the harlots of Babylon?
42). Why is Babylon blaspheming God?
43). Jesus states in Matthew 24:29, 30 that a "sign" will appear for all to see.
44). Where will the "sign" of Christ appear for all to see?
45). Immediately after what event will the "sign" of Christ appear?
46). In between what two events is the "sign" of Christ wedged in?
47). Where can we find the "sign" of Christ mentioned?
48). Describe the "sign" of Christ.
49). What effect will the appearance of the "sign" of Christ have upon the wicked people of the world?
50). After what literal event will the second coming of Christ take place?
51). What activities will take place when Christ comes the second time to planet earth?
52). What condition will the earth be in when Christ comes the 2nd time?
53). What would happen to the all of the wicked living?
54). What would happen to all of the righteous living?
55). What would happen to the sun and to planet earth when Christ returns to heaven with the redeemed? *Hint* Isaiah 24

BIBLIOGRAPHY

* 1   Mitanidis Philip *Moses Wrote About Me* BEEHIVE PUBLISHING HOUSE INC. 2013 edition , pp 247-257

** 2   Mitanidis Philip *Christians Headed Into the Time of Trouble* BEEHIVE PUBLISHING HOUSE INC. 2007 pp 166-168

*** 3   Adam Clarke, *Commentary on the Old Testament*, vol. iv, p.596, note on Daniel 7:25

**** 4   Albert Barnes, *Notes on Daniel*, p. 328, comment on Daniel 7:25

***** 5   *Manual of Christian Doctrine,* John Joseph McVey, 1914, p.123